ENCOUNTERING GOD

REFLECTIONS ON THE COURTSHIP LETTERS OF MY RELIGIOUS PARENTS

Mark Johnson

Published by EA Books, Inc.
EAbooksonline.com
ISBN: 978-1-941733-33-2

CONTENTS

BEGINNINGS

Walter met Margaret at a church outing when she visited
her sister in Greeley, Colorado, at summer's end, 1937.
Shortly afterwards, Margaret returned to Washburn, North
Dakota to direct choral groups and teach high school
English. Walter and Margaret married thirteen months later.
Aside from two brief visits, their courtship resides entirely in
their letters.

The intimate imaginings of these Victorian holdovers,
often cloaked in allusion and innuendo, though not racy, are
seldom dull, often humorous, and sometimes surprisingly
frank. When they express a concern, it will be at least four
days, but often five or six, before the mailman brings the
wanted envelope holding their lover's response.

The religious and cultural concerns raised in the letters
are a look into the life of two western farming communities
in the late 1930s as seen through the eyes of two evangelical
Swedish-Lutherans. The Great War of their childhood and
the Great Depression of their early twenties was still fresh in

their minds when the economy tanked and Hitler swept into Austria.

A few years later, I became the fourth of their eight children. I can speak to my parent's faith. God came across in their daily lives through worship, prayers, praise, and thankfulness. Possibly as a result, I grew up with a deep-seated awareness, but an unresolved sense, of God. I pondered the joy my parents found in each other in the midst of what appeared to be an unrelenting financial struggle. One day I asked Dad, "Why are you a Christian?" He replied, "When you can show me a better way to live, I'll consider that."

My parents' letters surfaced after their funerals. After finally bothering to browse them, I found that, years before I probed Dad with my question, he and mom had scripted answers and views that revealed the breadth and depth of the spiritual joys and challenges that invigorated their lives as Christians.

While attempting to keep the feel of the letters, I deleted paragraphs and parts of paragraphs that were mundane, repetitive, or otherwise uninteresting outside of my greater family. I added some related experiences and perspectives from my life and appended some self-exploratory questions at the end of each chapter.

In transcribing the hand-written letters into more easily readable type, I made numerous compromises. Strikeouts and insertion arrows were removed. Postscripts, which occasionally wind around the edges of their letters, were appended after their signatures. Otherwise, the wording of the letters was transcribed as written except for Walter's consistent misspelling of receive. Although the emotion conveyed through hand-written script was lost, some of the urgency in answering a letter was retained in the authoring dates and mailing postmarks. Thus you have in your hands the unedited and principal concerns of Walter and Margaret while they are getting to know each other. And you have their takes on each other, on life, and on God colored, occasionally, by the anecdotal remembrances, explanations, and musings of a dedicated scientist, intrigued seeker, and grateful son.

ENCOUNTERING

*W*alter knew that Margaret would be visiting her sister, the new pastor's wife, but it wasn't until she rose in front of the congregation and sang that he began thinking she might be the partner for which he had prayed so fervently.

He also knew a lot about her through prior conversations with her older sister whose grandparents came to America during the first Swedish migration. They settled in the rich farm land of Illinois and Minnesota shortly before the Civil War. Her parents, a pastoral team, had played leading roles in a number of midwestern and western Swedish-Lutheran communities. Two of her brothers were Lutheran pastors with three years of seminary training. Two of her sisters married pastors. Like her brothers and sisters, she graduated from college, was musically talented, and was accustomed to the amenities of town life. As a high school teacher, she enjoyed a steady salary and extended vacations.

Walter's father, on the other hand, came over as an indentured servant during the second major Swedish migration in the late eighteen hundreds. His father's fare to America was seven years of hard farm work for an English farmer while sleeping at night in a hay loft. His parents, now farming their own land, stopped speaking Swedish at home after he flunked the first grade — an embarrassment he later assuaged by skipping two grades. After high school, he helped his dad farm. He learned the caprices of disease and infestation, the weather, and the commodity markets. Moreover, he milked cows and fed livestock every day of the week and every week of the year. He was a "share-cropper" (to use an epithet I would later hear from a cousin on my mother's side) completing his second year of farming on his own.

All we know of Walter and Margaret's first meeting comes in a March 14th letter, "I didn't do anything to make you interested in me except that I prayed for someone to take me home from that Luther League picnic." We later find out that they went on two sightseeing excursions together before Margaret headed back to her teaching job in North Dakota.

We soon learn that God is intimately involved in who they are and what they are about. But surprising are the differences in how two individuals see and relate to the source of their being. In addition to learning more about each other, as potential soulmates they will be sharing how each sees and experiences God. The letters in this book cover the first five months of those encounters.

Your first encounter with Walter and Margaret will be colored by what you have just read. If you are to know and appreciate the nuances of their takes on life, you must get beyond that initial coloring, their first few letters, even their manner of speaking. To encounter their souls, you must delve into what they are experiencing and trying to express. It's all here, but it takes time and thought. As Margaret says to Walter in her fourth letter, "I realize that you don't know me very well."

Walter will reply, "And you do not know me very well."

WHEN I FEEL I HAVE CHOSEN GOD

While the letters in this chapter were written, readers of the Washburn Leader, including Margaret, learned in September that Margaret was one of the returning high school teachers and learned in October that neutral nations were protesting Japan's attack on Nanking. Readers of the Greeley Tribune, including Walter, learned in August there was a major battle in Shanghai, in September that Japan was blocking the rescue of Americans and was mobilizing for war in Russia, and in October that Roosevelt had said that America could not ignore these events

August 30, 1937.

Dear Margaret:

Writing letters has always been a difficult task for me. I do not know how to start one, I have trouble finishing them and I do not know what to put in between. I find that this tends to make my letters very brief.

I like to read the letters that Paul wrote better than any I have ever read. You are in no doubt about the author of the letter and you do not have to look to the end of the letter to find out. I shall copy his salutation and just as he wished Gods Grace and peace upon all of his friends so to hope that you may experience just such Grace and peace throughout this year and those to come

First of all I must tell you that I have had the pictures developed that we took in the Poudre canyon and on Cameron pass. I am sending three of them. The others were

August 30, 1937 [Postmarked AUG 31 10 AM Greeley, CO]

Dear Margaret:

Writing letters has always been a difficult task for me. I do not know how to start one. I have trouble finishing them and I do not know what to put in between. I find that this tends to make my letters very brief.

I like to read the letters that Paul [the New Testament apostle] wrote better than any I have ever read. You are in no doubt about the author of the letter and you do not have to look to the end of the letter to find out. I shall copy his salutation and just as he wished Gods Grace and peace upon all of his friends so I to hope that you may experience just such Grace and Peace throughout this year and those to come.

First of all I must tell you that I have had the pictures developed that we took in the Poudre Canyon and on Cameron Pass. I am sending three of them. The others were ruined. . . . There are also some pictures of the Medicine Bow Range in Wyoming where I was with Frank Lunn this last Thurs. and Fri.

It is a short range and quite high. (Med.Bow Pk) 12005 ft. This small range stands alone in a Large basin about 140 to 200 miles in dia. From the top of this peak you command a magnificent view of this vast basin with the sky line or horizon anywhere from 75 to 100 miles distant.

In the pictures you will see a few of the many beautiful lakes of which there are many in this region. We did not fish, but spent our time hiking and visiting. We visited a gold mine and this proved interesting altho somewhat scary. (It is very dark inside of old mother earth.) Most of this country is heavily forested with large and beautiful trees. Over 1 million dollars worth of lumber is taken out of this small region annually altho it has no value except as railroad ties and prop timbers for mines.

We slept under the moon and the stars at a altitude of 10,000 ft. The night was mild and very beautiful, with the dwarfed pine trees throwing many grotesque shadows about us. But we were tired after climbing the peak and did not mind the shadows. I hope that some day you may climb this peak and see this beautiful country.

Enough said concerning mountains. I have thought a great deal about a discussion we had one Friday evening concerning movies and their merits and whether or not there were any that we might attend. Now my opinion is worth less than two cents (some authority said this of the average opinion) and I am so imperfect and slow to accept His grace that I could not give advice.

Your knowledge is more complete than mine, so it is not necessary to say that Satan is very subtle and sometimes in a weak moment we are taken unawares. I am going to tell you of a remark which I heard a few years ago which caused me to stop going to pool halls unless absolutely necessary. This mother put it this way to an older son. It may not hurt you, but perhaps some of your younger bros. or his friends will see you come and go from there. Since you attend church regularly and profess to be a Christian they will naturally think that it is perfectly right to frequent such places. Nearly each one of us has some of these young friends who read the gospel thru us. . . . I believe that this is the best reason for not attending even good shows until the movie industry is cleaned up more than at present. It could be a very good and useful means of education if properly conducted. There are many interesting fields, where we may seek recreation for instance, music, various concerts and recitals although I know that in a small town they are few, except by radio.

This is a suggestion for you in your work. It seemed to me that you truly loved the outdoor life and nature study. Would it not be possible to organize a group perhaps of girls or both girls and boys to make Sat. afternoon trips, into the surrounding country. One could collect various specimens of plant, insect and animal life and classify them and name them.

Now Margaret I have set down my thots as they came. They are imperfect My grammar is imperfect and I am a poor writer especially when writing too fast. For all these I humbly apologize. To make a long story short I was impressed by your sincerity and oneness with Him. Altho I only knew you a few weeks I am sure I was not mistaken. I shall pray that you may ever continue in him and always be a light unto others. I hope that I may hear from you occasionally during the coming months. One more thing. You

spoke of confidence and often you discounted your own talents.
There is a good article on this in the Young Peoples paper for Aug.
22. If you can obtain it read it. It is by U. G. Montgomery and is
titled (Don't discount yourself).

Now I have a request to make. As you know my father went to
Calif. to visit one of my sisters. She came back with him. . . .If
possible I wish that you and she might exchange addresses and
correspond. I am sure it would be of a real help to her. I shall ask
her to write first if I get your address. I am sending this to Clarissa
but you will soon go to Washburn.

Yours in Christian Fellowship, Walter Johnson.

P.S. Please extend my greetings to your mother and sister.

The mother, whose remark Walter, my Dad, mentioned,
may have been his. His mother and father were founding
members of the Immanuel Lutheran Church. He was the
oldest of five children. He professed to be a Christian and
had stopped frequenting the pool hall in Eaton around the
time he graduated from high school.

Margaret's response, mistakenly given an August date,
was postmarked in September. It arrived after what must
have been for Walter a disconcerting second week.

Box #142
Washburn, North Dakota
August 14, 1937

Dear Walter,

"Peace be unto you that are in
Christ." I Peter 5:14
"Casting all your anxieties upon him,
because he careth for you." I Peter 5:7

These two Bible passages
I wish to give to you. They have given
me much strength. Its so easy
for me to carry my worries with
me that I need this second
verse daily. I wish to thank you
for wishing me grace and peace,
and especially to thank you for remembering me in prayer. It gives
me added strength in weakness,
when I recall that there are those
who remember me in prayer. God
takes the prayers and blesses me
in turn. I am also remembering
you in prayer to the One who is so
wonderful in caring for His own.

August [September] 14, 1937 [Postmarked SEP 14 3 — PM
Washburn, ND]

Dear Walter,

"Peace be unto you that are in Christ." I Peter 5:14. "Casting
all your anxieties upon him, because he careth for you." I Peter 5:7

These two Bible passages I wish to give to you. They have
given me much strength. It's so easy for me to carry my worries
with me that I need this second verse daily. I wish to thank you for
wishing me grace and peace, and especially to thank you for
remembering me in prayer. It gives me added strength in
weakness, when I recall that there are those who remember me in
prayer. God takes the prayers and blesses me in turn. I am also
remembering you in prayer to the One who is so wonderful in
caring for his own.

The pictures turned out fine. I think the background scenery of
the picture, where I am sitting on a wooden railing is marvelous.
How high was the altitude for the group picture? I am planning to
paste my snapshots in the Kodak album . . . . I should remember
what the altitude was but I am unable to. You must have had a
splendid time with your friend up in Med. Bow Range. If it was
similar to the beauty and coldness of the place where we walked up
not far from that sign on the Cameron Pass, I can imagine a little
of how you spent the night. That little stream of water was
beautiful.

Thanks for the pamphlets too. It was interesting to look them through while riding on the bus out to Washburn. It was impossible for me to get a hold of the article "Don't Discount Yourself." I'll have to try to imagine its contents and strive to do my best.

Two of the teachers who are rooming at Jefferis with Helen and I, went to the theatre this evening. I am so thankful they didn't ask me to go along. Three of us lady teachers do not play bridge. We were all invited to a dinner and card party but we asked to be excused from playing cards. They were so friendly to us and furnished us with other entertainment and then Helen and I finished the remainder of the time sewing and knitting. It was lots of fun. I hope that we might be witnesses for Christ.

This year I am teaching all four years of high school English. Mr. Thorson asked me which I preferred English II or Latin I. I told him English so that is how it turned out. Then this evening I found out that I am to have charge of the Boys and Girls Glee Clubs and the Mixed Chorus. Mr. Thorson is so very kind to me because now I won't have to keep on practicing after four and at night. Eight of the teachers are educated in music so he is dividing up the practicing. Some have charge of trios; others of quartets; and still others, of solos. Now I will have more time to keep up my practice on voice, piano and flute. I surely appreciate it. There aren't very many superintendents as thoughtful and kind as he.

Walter, tell your sister that I would enjoy writing to her. I wish that I could have met her. . . . If I can help her in any way I will be glad to do so.

How are the sugar beets getting along? I presume they are soon ready for harvest. It perhaps is unnecessary now.

Thank you for showing me the mountains. May He help me to visualize all that He has made for me to enjoy.

May God bless you,

Margaret.

Although Margaret was far from intimate and didn't acknowledge his suggestion on collecting and classifying "plant, insect and animal life," she wasn't discouraging. She asked about his sugar beets and planned to paste his snapshots in her photo album. Walter responded eight days later.

Sept. 22 [SEP 24 430 PM]

Dear Margaret:

Tonight as I begin to write, I am very thankful and grateful to God, for your friendship and for the friendship of my other Christian friends: My prayer shall ever be, that His Grace and Peace shall ever be yours.

I thank you for the verses that you sent to me. I am sending one that helps me to meet many trials, especially when I begin to feel my burdens and feel that God is giving me more than my share. "Ye did not choose me, but I chose you, and appointed you that ye should go and bear fruit, and that your fruit should abide: that whatsoever ye shall ask of the Father in my name, He may give it to you." John 15:16.

When I feel that I have chosen God, so that I might experience his peace and salvation; it is good for me to remember this verse. I feel that by these little trials and obstacles I am being guided and kept in the way by Him.

If you will pardon me for mentioning it again, I shall write a few words concerning shows and other so called amusements. Perhaps I am too serious and let my mind dwell on it too much. It is not of myself that I am thinking for I know I do not care for them even if it were not a religious principle. My S. S. [Sunday school] class is a group of boys between 14 & 18 yrs. of age and this question, naturally comes up quite often. It does not seem right to

me, to tell them that these things are all wrong and then not offer
them something else, which would be better to do. . . . (I wonder
how Paul took care of this. I believe in prayer.) but surely there are
many worthwhile things to do . . . such as hiking, nature study
and many other things.

Fall is coming on very fast. The mornings are cold and the
leaves on the trees are turning. Sometimes I shudder when I think
of the cold creeping on. But I rejoice to think that next spring new
life will flow thru the trees again just as we will experience new life
after we have passed thru that cold shadow which always leaves us
cold when we think of it.

Time is passing swiftly and I must close this letter again
thanking Him for Christian friends and fellowship.

May His Grace and Peace Abide with you,
Walter

I have read that in the mating ritual of cardinals the male
gives a seed to the female. Margaret began her letter by
giving a Bible verse to Walter. Walter responded in kind — a
spiritual kiss they would share at the opening of each letter

October 3 [OCT 5 3--PM]

Dear Walter,

"Jehovah is gracious and merciful; Slow to anger, and of great loving kindness. Jehovah is good to all; And His tender mercies are over all His works." Psalm 145: 8, 9.

This morning the sun is shining so brightly and the wind is blowing just enough to make the weather ideal. I think there is a verse in the Bible which says "This is the Lord's day we should be glad and rejoice in it." It happens that it is Sunday so I can fully enjoy nature.

This evening I had the chance to sing a solo at the Methodist church. Perhaps you know the selection, "A Divine Redeemer" by Gounod. That was the number. I have never been able to sing it as easily before. God answered my prayer.

I need to be reminded of the waste of time, money, and sin of seeing movies. I have seen Prince and the Pauper by Mark Twain since I have been to Washburn. I believe that picture was all right. The teachers seem to think most any picture is okay. Walter, it isn't always easy to refuse but one certainly feels at peace after refusing.

So many have asked me if I dance. When I answer in the negative they usually add why don't you; do you think it sin or just can't you. It seems the only pleasure some folks enjoy is on the dance floor, in the theatre, or at the card table. I, too, have often

21

wondered how Paul solved the pleasure problem. I think it fine that you are helping your Sunday School to find enjoyment in different ways.

Poor English IV class have a one thousand word short story to hand in tomorrow morning. Today they reported on their titles and dominant incidents. I believe their compositions are going to be very good. In English II we are studying Emerson's essays. I just can't understand how you could pass with a 98% grade in the subject which you mentioned, without at least studying from the text at one time before six weeks' tests. You surely must have listened attentively. My ability doesn't come up to your standard. If you could have gone to college, you would have gotten more out of it than I did.

Your harvest season is very long. I presume the hours of work are many and long also. The poor farmers around here had very little to harvest. Helen's father got no crop whatever.

May you continue in your work for Him.

Yours in Christ,

Margaret

There is something within each of us that can sense — without any teaching — when things do or don't sit right with us. That something is manifest in a just-delivered baby when its cries are silenced by its mother's arms.

That something is like a tuning fork with sounding boards that pick up and amplify its harmonies when circumstances appropriately coalesce. Our tuning forks and their sounding boards develop in a most natural manner when we are children lost in play and surrounded by love. Later the harmonies grow richer and more robust when we find enduring joys and meanings in life. I don't know that we can ever fully lose a tuning fork, but like our conscience, our sounding boards can be dampened, ignored, or even suppressed over extended periods of time. Peers can pressure, commitments overwhelm, successes lead astray, failures dull hope, and fears cramp vision to the point that we can be left wondering if there is not more to life than what we are experiencing.

Finding activities that resonate with our sounding boards of joy can be a soul-searching effort. Many things come into play. Consider Margaret's simple statement, "It is Sunday so I can fully enjoy nature." Others may not enjoy nature. That's OK; enjoying nature resonated for Margaret. Others may anticipate weekdays or weekends. Sunday worked for her. The specifics and activities, which vary from person to person, are not critical so long as periods of settled

joy are a normal and recurring feature of our lives, especially
when we are surrounded by concerns and conflicting
desires.

Walter was encouraged, no doubt, by Margaret's
rejoicing in "the Lord's day," enjoying nature, and
appreciating his Emersonian acumen. The phrase "poor
farmers" would have also caught his eye. Allowing for the
two or three days it took for the mail to travel from
Washburn to Greeley, Walter lost no time in responding.

Oct. 7 [OCT 8 430 PM]

Dear Margaret:

"When I consider the heavens, the works of thy fingers, The moon and the stars which thou has ordained; What is man, that thou art mindful of him? And the son of man, that thou visitest him?" Psalm 8: 3,4

I have so many things to be thankful for today. As I took a short walk after supper, to thank Him for my many blessings, I wondered at the fact that he is mindful of me. But I remember that we are told "in the 12th Chap of Luke the 7th verse" that even the hairs of our heads are numbered.

Tomorrow we will finish digging potatoes on my place. ("I am working together with my father and brother.") They have been fairly good. All the other crops were good. I also got 25 head of very good cattle to feed thru this winter. (We buy this stock in the fall, feed it thru the winter and sell it in the spring at a profit we hope.) At present I am thankful for, what seems to be a fortunate purchase. Then on top of all this comes your welcome and inspiring letter. Thank you, for it and the verse you sent. It fitted my thot for tonight so very well. I am sure that you must admit, that I have much to be thankful for. I pray, that I may at least be thankful, for I can never be worthy of these blessings.

The Denver Post reported heifers, a volatile commodity, selling at $12.25 to $13.25 on August 16. Roughly, two weeks later, heifers sold for $8.50 to $12.50. Walter purchased his heifers sometime in the interim during a serendipitous dip in the price. He would fatten them over winter and sell them in time for the spring field work. He could expect heifer prices to recover by then for him to make a handsome profit.

After services last Sunday Robert Johnson and I drove to the top of the Trail ridge road, (12183 ft) and back to Greeley. . . . The aspen, the woodvine and small shrubbery were beautiful in their many colored hues. As we were coming down we saw the beautiful sunset. I wish that you might have been along and enjoyed the whole trip but especially as we came into one of the parks just above Estes Park. There we saw a large herd of elk feeding and the bugle of the bull elks is a sound I shall never forget. It is actually beautiful and very musical. There were perhaps 25 cars and a hundred people watching them but they were very unconcerned. Farther down we saw more elk and numerous deer.

At one time last Sunday I thot that Margaret would enjoy seeing something like this once in a while. It is certainly too bad that there is nothing to see in N.D. But I said No Walt your wrong! You know that you like the great plains also and as I looked at the map I knew that you must be near the great Missouri river and that upon its banks and near it you must find some of the scenery that you describe in your letter and picture. The great bank in the picture looks very much as it did when I saw it in Pierre, S.D.

You tell of studing Emerson in English class and let me say here and now that it was harder for me than any other subject. I should never have boasted but my 98 without study was in Commercial Geography.

I know that a prayer uttered with respect for the will of our Heavenly Father is always answered and I know that He helped you last Sunday.

May He ever be your guide and help and may His Grace and Peace be yours.

Walter

What we see and experience depends so much on our understanding of what is out there. This fact was forcefully driven home one day after I returned from an extended vacation with my family. A metal storm window lay unbroken on the ground partially covered by some leaves and other debris. I knelt down and, after carefully scratching about the debris, soon found the two metal hinges needed to rehang it.

I mounted the window, but when closing it, I realized the L-shaped fasteners and their corresponding nuts for holding the window shut were missing. After carefully scratching through the dirt and debris again, I found the fasteners and the wing nuts — struck by having overlooked them in the first place.

I installed the latches. The storm window, now held closed, jiggled against the mounting frame. Then I remembered the springs needed to take up the slack. Down I went again and soon found the springs in the same bits of leaves and dirt.

In each case I quickly found what I was looking for. When looking for hinges, I found hinges; when looking for fasteners and nuts, I found fasteners and nuts; when looking for springs, I found springs.

Our takes on life are mental glasses that bear heavily on what we look for and find. Walter saw a caring world in which even the hairs on his head were taken into account.

October 17 [OCT 18 7 – AM]

Dear Walter,

The work of teaching is lots of fun, but at the end of a six weeks period it gets rather trying as there seems to be so much to do. This time I wrote my texts on the typewriter using stencils so that they could be mimeographed. It has helped me to have studied typing this past summer.

Walter, this morning the S. S. superintendent asked me to teach the young peoples' Bible class. I declined because it takes a lot of preparation and I do enjoy having Sunday be one when I can drink in knowledge rather than give out and also because I like to go to our Augustana Lutheran services at Wilton and North Underwood. I have charge of the Junior Choir and then I belong to the Senior Choir. The superintendent said that he would ask the pastor to teach the class instead. The pastor has but one congregation so I don't think that would be asking too much and, furthermore, he would perhaps prefer having charge of the class.

It must have been fun to travel up the mountains in the fall of the year. The trees were no doubt grand in their myriads of autumn colors. The pine was still green which must have been even more striking because of the contrast of color. To think that you got to hear the bugle call of the bull elk. I asked Mr. Thorson what the sound was like. He said that it resembled the coyote's call but that [it] was deeper and more sonorous. Was he right?

Mr. Thorson's comparison of an elk's bugle with a coyote's yelp puzzled me. A bull elk's bugling is musical; so is a coyote's yelping. The similarity ends there, as I found out one midnight while setting water at the top of a bean field.

Waking up in the middle of the night to irrigate another part of a field was never pleasant. Driving the pickup to the top of the field was fun, but once you turned off the engine, closed the door, and grabbed your shovel, you were alone except for a couple of yard lights flickering over a half mile away.

Once at work changing a set of water on a quiet night, the surrounding peace and solitude would eventually engulf me: the moon playing hide-and-seek with the clouds, a gently stirring breeze, water gurgling down the cuts in the ditch banks, crickets chirping, an occasional frog croaking, boots crunching the clay curls left from dried-up mud puddles. That solitude was split one midnight by a coyote's shrill, piercing yelps ascending a spine-tingling scale in staccato sixteenths. I turned and swung my shovel—nothing there, only the bean leaves flickering in the moonlight. After that chilling frisson, those midnight solitudes were never quite the same.

I am glad that you decided that the scenery in North Dakota is beautiful in its way. Marie Nesting and I were down to the river the other evening. The moon was shining down over the water so that it made a golden path across the river. I wish that I could have walked right across it.

Well, now it is time for me to retire. Tomorrow I must get busy averaging marks. I hope and pray that I will give the pupils their deserved grade. May God bless and keep you and may you continue walking in His steps.

Yours in Christ,

Margaret

Margaret's wanting time for herself reminded me of an enigmatic teaching of Jesus in Luke 10:38-42:

> *Now as they went on their way, he entered a village; and a woman named Martha received him into her house. And she had a sister called Mary, who sat at the Lord's feet and listened to his teaching. But Martha was distracted with much serving; and she went to him and said, "Lord, do you not care that my sister has left me to serve alone? Tell her then to help me." But the Lord answered her, "Martha, Martha, you are anxious and troubled about many things;*

31

one thing is needful. Mary has chosen the good portion,
which shall not be taken from her."

In this story Martha (who welcomed Jesus) was
concerned (Jesus felt she was distracted) about being a good
hostess (for which her friends may have praised her). She felt
Mary was ignoring her duties as a hostess and selfishly
attending to her personal interests. Mary, on the other hand,
was in touch with something Jesus saw as needful. (I believe
it was her joy, and, should she find it, she would more likely
be envied than praised.) Jesus pointed out that what Mary
sought would not be taken from her.

Jesus could have praised Martha for helping the guests
enjoy themselves. The guests might have applauded. Martha
probably would have felt much better, but can the praise of
others really resonate with your deep joy when you would be
elsewhere?

Something in the presence and voice of Jesus evidently
silenced for Mary the tiresome drumming of duty and the
distracting clamor of desire for at least one precious moment.
Maybe she felt a satisfying shift in who she was and what she
was about.

Self-insistence differs profoundly from selfishness when
seeking the source of one's true joy. Margaret would have
received praise—or at least a hearty thanks—for agreeing to
teach the young peoples' Bible class. Instead she insisted that

Sunday be a time for revitalization rather than another day filled with additional commitments.

A GLIMPSE BACK

My parents enjoyed life in the midst of struggle. That joy comes across in their letters. Ferreting out the keys to someone's joy can be a rewarding task. What one looks for and eventually finds often begins with a question. Here are some self-exploratory questions tied to the letters of Walter and Margaret. There are no "right" answers. There are only your answers, for you are the world's authority on how you see things — and on what you look for and what you find in how others see things.

August 30. Prior to meeting Margaret, writing letters had been a difficult task for Walter. Something about Margaret started the words flowing for Walter. What is the nature of those things that start the words flowing for you?

September 14. Margaret chose not to participate with her friends in an activity she felt was morally questionable. How do you see the moral choices of your friends influencing your choices?

September 22. Walter thanked Margaret for the Bible verses she sent in her first letter and returned a verse that meant a lot to him. How might their exchanging of Bible verses contribute to their spiritual intimacy? What ways have helped you establish spiritual intimacy with another person?

October 3. Margaret looked forward to enjoying nature on Sunday afternoons. What regular times and activities of the day or week bring assured enjoyment to your life?

October 7. Walter was thankful for the "starry heavens." How does your view of what is going on in your world affect your thankfulness for what you see?

October 17. How do you see the difference between self-insistence and selfishness? Can you recall times when you embraced you "inner Mary?" What happened when you did?

THE POTTER'S HANDS

Readers of the October 25 edition of the Greeley Tribune learned of Japan's declaration to "Strike at Russia."

Oct. 25 [OCT 26 430 PM]

Dear Margaret:

Brethren, I count not myself yet to have laid hold; but one thing I do, forgetting the things which are behind, and stretching forward to the things which are before, I press on toward the goal unto the prize of the high calling of God in Christ Jesus. Phil. 3:13,14.

It is some consolation in knowing that Paul too, had moments in which he felt insufficient. There is so much to be done, so many things I could do, if only I could develop the spirit and be master of my own flesh. This weakness grieves me a great deal.

I wish that I might assure you that I am praying for you in your work and all walk of life. It would indeed be a joy to see you and visit with you. It is always a joy for me to visit with my Christian friends and I thank God for each one of them. North

Dakota is a long way from here and at best it will be a long while before I may have that privilege. If it is his will I will be hoping that it may not be too long.

Mr. Thorson's description of the elks call is very good altho I might say that if you were alone and heard a coyote call it would cause you to pause and shudder, then quicken your step, while the call of the elk causes you to stop and strain to hear it again. I believe this would be true even though you had never heard either one before.

Margaret I noticed your decision concerning the teaching of S. S. Class. I am sure that you were guided, by the one who can direct us rightly. It is not good to assume so many duties that we have to slight some of them. You must be very busy with the program that you have already and you should be thankful for it. There is time enough to assume more tasks as His Grace permits us to.

Now, may the Grace and Peace of God; be with you on the Way everlasting.

Walter

Oct. 30 [OCT 31 3 PM]

Dear Margaret:

"Grace and Peace; be unto you from God our Father."

"If you abide in my word, then are you truly my disciples, and ye shall know the truth, and the truth shall make you free." Jn. 8:31,32.

Freedom: Our nation fought the revolutionary war to gain religious and political freedom. We fought to free the slaves from their bondage. Theodore Roosevelt fought to free us from the bondage of great trusts being organized at that time. Women fought for the right to vote. Today they are fighting for equality with men in all things. We hear on all sides of us, concerning moral freedom of the younger generation.

With all this freedom; is it not irony, that each day, we are becoming more deeply enmeshed in the greatest bondage that ever afflicted men, Sin; We see it on all sides, we know how cruelly it holds us from the thing that we desire most of all, Freedom.

As I read that verse tonight, many questions became more clear to me than ever before. I know that it is not enough that I go to church each Sunday, that I teach in the Sunday school, Sing in the Choir [Dad tried his best to sing when Mom asked.] and occasionally force myself to visit the sick and needy.

I said above; force myself to do these things. Many, many of us do these things because we feel duty bound or perhaps we think that in that way we become justified. Sometimes these activities become a joy and are a joy but not always, at least for the great majority of us. Why is it? We do not abide in His word and in Him enough. That must always be first and come first. Then as we experience the knowledge of the truth and the freedom, "that is;" freedom from the bondage of Sin; We will at all times joyously visit the sick and needy, clothe the naked and feed the hungry.

Margaret: why did I perhaps bother you and may ?? bore you with my thought. I know that you are busy and shall not ask you to spend too much of your time trying to follow me. Nevertheless I am going to dare to hope that you may wish to correct me if you see this in a better light and I shall even dare to hope that you will exchange meditations with me. Often I gain a better insight thru an exchange of thots with my friends.

Now I pray, that you may experience the greater freedom.
Yours in Christ,

Walter

Interestingly, Walter didn't want to break free from visiting the sick and needy. He wanted to break free from whatever was keeping him from enjoying it.

October 30 [NOV 1 7 – AM]

Dear Walter,

"But seek ye first his kingdom, and his righteousness; and all these things shall be added unto you." Matthew 6:33.

Thanks for the letter which I received. I can imagine that you are very busy. I thought I would be right in writing you now as letters are encouraging at times. Don't work too hard, tho.

The convention was pretty good. There were some over 21,000 teachers attending. Quite a number of the teachers haven't received their full salary because of lack of funds. I have certainly been fortunate in always getting mine.

Walter, I am so happy because I met with one teacher, who seemed so discouraged, whom I had the chance to have devotions with. She teaches in a rural school near Esmond. She said that she had met with a terrible accident some years previous. . . . She is a Lutheran girl who rooms and boards in a Catholic home and teaches in a Catholic community. She said she hadn't read much in her Bible and she thought maybe that was the reason she was having so much trouble. We are planning to write letters to one another.

Walter, I wish you didn't live so far away too because it would be lots of fun to be with you. I would truly have enjoyed being with you up the Trail Ridge Road. I realize that you don't know me very well, but if God wants you to know me better He will so arrange

41

but, if not, He will hinder it. I want to be as clay in the Potter's hands. Oh that He would mold me and make me after his will. Thank you for remembering me in prayer. It sustains me to have prayers uttered in my behalf. I can still feel that the prayers my father uttered for me while he was living are still being answered. Christians can be a wonderful help to one another thru the medium of prayer.

Margaret has prepared a sandwich for Walter that may take some chewing. The two outside layers are fine. She enjoyed being with him and appreciated his prayers. The meat may be a problem. The Potter could have other plans for her life, and that would be fine with her.

Margaret could have used a river metaphor: "going with the flow," or a fate metaphor: "whatever will be, will be." Instead she related what she saw through a theistic metaphor.

One time during the convention I just felt such an urge to prayer that I left everything and returned to my room in the hotel. Now I realize why it was. Later in the afternoon I met that lonely teacher of whom I have spoken. Poor girl she had gotten into an awful hotel; the room was dirty as well as high-priced; the key that fit her door was used by all the roomers; then, too it was quite a distance from the high school building, where our meetings were held. I am so glad that I could help her out. She said that both men and women were drinking liquor at the place where she was staying. I certainly realize that God directed me to a clean hotel. It also happened that about six o'clock of the same day, as I was with this girl, I saw County Supt. Peterson and his wife riding in their car. We were just going to cross the street over to my rooming place when Petersons' car had to stop because of the heavy traffic. I just felt like I should ask to ride home with them after the evening's program. I hesitated, finally, I decided, if their car stops because of the engine's not being cared for just right after they have once started I am to speak to them. Well, it so happened. They told me that I was welcome but that I might have to ride a little uncomfortably as three others were to ride with them. I hurriedly returned to my room, packed my things and, wrote a little note to the three teachers with whom I was staying, that I was to leave for Washburn half an hour after the concert. Well, was I surprised, when I returned to get my things after the concert, to see the girls busy packing. They said that they, too, were to ride with Petersons'. They had planned to stay for the ball but decided that it was wiser to return home and thus save money. After I returned home I found that my money would not have reached to pay for another night's lodging, meals, and bus fare. God knew that I was in need but I didn't realize it. He helped me out.

Now I must go to sleep . . . . May God bless and keep you.

Sincerely,

Margaret

Naturally Margaret's mind sought an explanation for the surprising coordination she experienced. She didn't attribute it to Lady Luck or to her sagacity. Instead she saw God taking her thoughts and needs into account.

The Bible speaks of the God of Abraham, the God of Isaac, and the God of Jacob. That expression appeals to me. In the plain sense of the text, the same god is being referenced; however, what we see and experience of the workings of God depends greatly on our "God sense." The God of Margaret was intimately involved in her daily affairs.

Nov 6 [NOV 7 230 PM]

Dear Margaret:

Margaret: You thought, that a letter at the time you wrote, would be encouraging. How Much: You may not know for a surety, altho sometimes it seems, that there is some tie that binds even tho the distance may be great.

It is sad about the young teacher you mentioned.

Margaret; It is true that I do not know you very well, as you said: and you do not know me very well. I too would be pliable; so that He may mold me into a useful part of His great plan.

Margaret; as I go about my work each day I often ponder upon many things. I have often pondered upon what Love, Marriage and the Home really are.

God is love: I do not know exactly at this moment where this is found. But I do know that at all times God expressed Himself in service, kindness and in gentle consideration of His people. And so I think that all true love is so expressed. We thank God for our emotions, they are gifts from him. But we must also ask his help in controlling our expression of them. The emotions of a Christian, Guided by God's true love: must surely be deeper, kinder, more considerate and more enduring than those that are not.

The many broken homes and marriages of today, point to the fact, that the young people of this land, express their emotions with little thought of true love, as God would have us love.

God also said; To suffer little children to come unto him. It is a shame that they are given so little consideration, but left by the parents to be brought up in an institution or by foster parents.

True love; whether between two men, two women or a man and a woman, must surely be a culmination of true friendship and understanding and as such, cannot be realized instantly.

Thank you; Margaret, for your letter and all that was in it.

May god keep you and Nourish you, so that you may grow in Knowledge, Truth and Grace.

Walter

Given the moral climate of today regarding homosexuality, much can be read into Walter's comment regarding true love between "two men, two women or a man and a woman." Although I don't remember either Mom or Dad ever discussing the subject, Lois, one of my sisters, recalled Mother telling her about the following incident in our church.

Leonard Jones [not his real name] got up at a meeting of the congregation and said that he was a homosexual (or she may have said gay), and that he would resign if the congregation was uncomfortable with his being the organist (she may have said choir director). I immediately got up and said, "Leonard, you were baptized in this church. You were confirmed in this church. You are a member of this church. And you are welcome in this church."   After that, no one said anything.

Walter commented on the encouragement he received in Margaret's letters. He mentioned the teacher she met at the convention. He too wanted to be "pliable," yet when Margaret pointed out how God miraculously arranged her transportation back from the convention, he had nothing to say. Can this be an oversight, or was it for him simply a happy coincidence? By a similar token, Margaret failed to acknowledge the auspiciousness of Walter's fortuitous cattle purchase. Did she not see God's hand in it, or did she not want to counter Walter's seeing his good buy as fortuitous?

November 6 [NOV 6 3 – PM]

Dear Walter,

Beloved, now are we the Sons of God, and it doth not yet appear what we shall be: but we know that, when he shall appear, we shall be like him; for we shall see him as he is. I John 3:2.

I, even I, and he that blotteth out thy transgressions for my own sake, and will not remember thy sins. Isaiah 43:25.

These two gems are so wonderful that it is hard for me to grasp enough of them. Such truths I wish more people would possess. When I think that if I continue to let God always be my protector, guide, and upholder I shall someday be like Him everything changes to happiness. After I have sinned and have prayed for forgiveness the second verse gives me much joy, since I know, it is for Christ's own sake I am forgiven. May I help others to receive the wonderful assurance of forgiveness of sins and life everlasting with Christ. But Jesus knows that the cares of this life often puts a veil between me and Him. May I live in Him then the cares are all cast upon Him and the veil is broken.

That I was loved as a child of God came through virtually unquestioned in my interpretation of the Bible and the love of my parents. My siblings, along with my small size, ensured this inherent sense of self-worth didn't morph into a superiority complex. Although I displeased my parents many times, I could not walk beyond their love, much less the love of God. Somehow I knew God and my parents always wanted me back.

Walter, I am so glad that you enjoy things that are spiritual and I truly thank you for wishing the gifts of His grace and peace to be mine. Those two gifts from God are better than anything that I know because they are really the greatest of riches. Now, I want God to grant you His peace and grace, which you may receive in Christ.

The Girls Glee Club is to sing at an Armistice program this coming Thursday. They are thrilled about it. The song is "To a Wild Rose" by MacDowell. [The song has a hauntingly peaceful lyric.]

Last night the Freshmen class return party was held. The pupils were even more wound up than at the last party. How they did enjoy playing Skip to My Lou! Some of [the] pupils started dancing on the stage back of the stage scenery. Mr. Thorson announced to everyone, "If you're going to dance, come out in the open, but you're not dancing here." After he had left about fourteen of the pupils came up to Helen and asked if they might dance now. She answered in the negative and they seemed satisfied to play the Needle's Eye instead.

Yours in Christ,

Margaret

Mr. Thorson's announcement brought back a time my two older brothers and I decided to give smoking a whirl. We picked up some unfinished cigarette butts along the side of the country road on our mile-and-a-quarter walk from grade school.

The next morning we commandeered a few matches and huddled behind the garage. We had each lit up a cigarette butt and were puffing and coughing when Dad's footsteps sounded on the gravel just around the corner. We froze, sheepishly fingering the evidence.

"What are you doing piddling around? You should have been finished with the chores a half hour ago." Silence. He looked into each of us or at least into me. "If you are going to smoke, don't hide behind some building. Smoke out in the open like a man, and if you need cigarettes, I'll buy them for you."

He left, and with him left my thought that smoking cigarettes was manly.

A GLIMPSE BACK

October 25. How would you characterize the support Walter gave Margaret concerning her decision not to teach the Sunday school class?

October 30. Walter "occasionally forced himself to visit the sick and the needy." Do you ever feel your joy in helping someone depends how closely you identify with the need of that person and whether or not you see that individual as a friend, stranger, enemy or as a fellow human?

Walter also said that "sometimes these activities are a joy, but not always," before asking, "Why is that?" He felt it was because we did not "abide in His word and in Him enough." What helps you identify more with the people you are trying to help?

October 30. Margaret used a potter metaphor to convey how she saw her life unfolding with Walter. What words might you use in a similar circumstance? Going with the flow? Whatever will be, will be?

November 6. Walter felt that true love was expressed in "service, kindness, and gentle consideration." Would you agree? If not, what is your definition of true love?

Using your definition of true love, do you feel that many homes break up because they are not based on true love? If so, why might a couple build a home on something other than true love?

November 6. Margaret found two "gems" on how to view herself. What are some of many ways people view themselves? How do see these ways affecting how they experience their world?

THE CLOUDS OF WAR

The November 11 issue of the Greeley Tribune noted that fifteen hundred paraded for peace on Armistice Day. Nine days later the Washburn Leader reported the country's concern that Fascists were invading Latin America. Heifers sold from $7 to $10.25 on the fifteenth.

November 11 [NOV 11 3 – PM]

Dear Walter,

Today we had an Armistice program at school. The speaker told of the horrors of war and then mentioned that the clouds of war are lowering over us. It rather worried me. I can't understand why people are unable to live peaceably together but then I realize that I get angry and say cutting remarks that can cause hurt feelings so it is only God can help humanity thru the peace of Christ to live harmoniously together.

This coming Saturday evening the "School-masters" (The title rather amuses me.) of this county are to have a banquet at Max. I have never attended so I plan to this time.

Walter, I just don't know what to write or how to express myself in regard to the last part of your letter. I do believe that God does want His children to love one another, to be wedded into a holy matrimony, and to build and maintain Christian homes. I believe that is his holy plan of continuing the Christian race. I have had a Christian home for which I truly thank God. It is sad to see and think of what condition unchristian families live in. But it is a joy to see a family who has the Unseen Guest always in their home. Peace and Love reign supreme and the result is happiness.

I haven't received any letter from your sister but I realize that she hasn't known me at all so I don't blame her. Maybe what I would write would be misguiding her. Walter, I believe you can help her more if I wouldn't write to her.

May God continue to bless and keep you for him.

Yours in His service,

Margaret

Interestingly, Margaret looked for how she might have contributed to the world's turmoil. She saw anger, an emotion she has felt, as one of the issues, and was concerned that sometimes, when she was angry, she made cutting remarks.

Such small things — how can cutting remarks contribute to a world problem? It is like asking how droplets from foggy mists can ever give rise to a mighty river. The analogy is soft. Cutting remarks are needles that pierce and stick, and when they do, they can become a part of you and get passed on. Worse, they can muffle, and even silence, a sounding board of joy by the mental scabbing that can result. Here is how Jesus in Matthew 5:22 views these little stilettos:

> *You have heard that it was said to the men of old, "You shall not kill; and whoever kills shall be liable to judgment." But I say to you that everyone who is angry with his brother shall be liable to judgment; whoever insults his brother shall be liable to the council, and whoever says, "You fool!" shall be liable to the hell of fire.*

Helplessness and hopelessness naturally follow when we focus on the failures of others and concentrate on causes that we can do nothing about. Uncovering even a sliver of personal responsibility, as Margaret did here, increases the likelihood of experiencing the joy of seeing how we might be empowered to help.

Nov. 11[NOV 12 430 PM]

Dear Margaret,

These things have I spoken unto you, that in me you may have peace. John 16: 33.

Nineteen years ago, we all felt, that we would have peace in the world. To most of us, the signing of the armistice meant peace. Long before, even the beginning of this war and others Christ spoke the words above. It is sad that we must ever seek the hard way. Our statesmen, seemingly rack their brains for a way to promote peace. I wonder if it is a confidence, in our own ability which causes us to overlook the simple way that our savior offered.

Margaret, I thank you for the verses you send and especially your prayers; I need them. They are like a helping hand in a rough mt. path. I remember that I took your hand, when we followed the little stream upon Cameron Pass thinking it might help you. But, it was I that stumbled and needed a helping hand as we came down.

Since the harvest is over I have started rising early enough to allow me at least one half hour in communion with Him and in His word. First upon arising, I go to an open window and breathe deeply with clean fresh air. Then I do a routine of exercises which help to keep the body fit and supple. God has granted me strength and health and I feel it my duty to maintain it to the best of my ability. After these exercises I am well awakened and I can truly

enjoy a few minutes of study, meditation and communion with
Him. . . . It was hard to begin getting up an hour earlier but I
asked God to help me and it became easier, but I am as yet very
weak. Nevertheless I already feel much better, even physically and
I feel much nearer to Him.

If I had your permission and could make the necessary
arrangements, "financial and arrangements to get the necessary
work done", I should like very much to visit with you in your
house during the Christmas Vacation. I am not worthy of the
privilege, yet I cannot restrain myself from asking it, if it can be
made possible. May His will be done in this matter.

Yours in Christ,

Walter

How quickly the cost-to-benefit ratios of exercise reveal
their discouraging faces. Walter tabulated some benefits: a fit
and flexible body, strength and health, feeling physically
and spiritually refreshed. He didn't mention Margaret by his
side, but that would have been an easily imagined and
rewarding image. He also felt he would need some
assistance with the substantial cost: rising an hour earlier.

Nov. 18 [NOV 18 10 PM]

Dear Margaret:

Train up a child in the way he should go, and even when he is old he will not depart from it. Prov: 22,6.

It is not hard to see and understand that; Rev and Mrs. Leaf had this in mind, when they bro't up their children. Out of their training and written word, which you learned to read, speak and write you have a true wisdom and knowledge.

You were bemoaning your letter writing, especially the example that you set as an English teacher. What you said may be true, for I do not know, my knowledge of English grammar and letter writing is very limited. But this I do know; that if we overlook the grammar part (you'll have to do that with my letters), your letters contain messages of thot, wisdom and rich knowledge which you get from your daily contact with Him. I enjoy them so very much. There is so much encouragement in them. Only one thing, do I fear; that you have so much work to do that they may make an extra burden upon you. Margaret; I know that after all, any written word is cold and I fear that I do not make myself very clear.

When I asked you to write to my sister I did not think of the fact that you are very busy. Nevertheless I also know that, that was not the reason that you suggested that I try to help her. It is very hard sometimes to know what to say; how much and what shall it be. May He be our guide, if we should have cause to counsel anyone.

From your last letter, I can easily see that you are quite busy; what with band practice, "School-Masters" banquets, choir practice and learning to knit. I am afraid that I must draw the line at knitting, my knowledge of that art is so scant; so very scant.

Concerning war; our armistice day programs seem a farce to me. We talk of peace and prepare for war. The way to educate for peace, is as you say, with God's help and thru his word. Only He can so instill love in our hearts, that we will not desire to war against our fellowmen, but will love them and share with them, our many blessings thru Him our Savior.

Speaking of literature; there is now on the market a book, by Dale Carnegie [How to Win Friends and Influence People], that is certainly worth any ones time and thought. Over 600,000 copies have been sold, so I am sure you can obtain a copy, if not I should be happy to send mine to you.

Yours in Christ.

Walter

My childhood questions and understandings were never belittled by Mom and Dad. I could explore the reasons for their decisions. Of course when questioning chores or work, the discussion occasionally ended with "Because I told you so."

Years later while working toward a master's degree in statistics, I drove a kindly professor to distraction arguing over the convergence of a particular numerical series. We had only intuitive arguments. He could have told me to come back when I had a mathematical proof. Instead he said, "When you get your Ph.D, you can argue with me" — his version of "because I told you so."

I was dumbfounded. I did not see how a professor with a Ph. D. and I, without one, had anything to do with the persuasiveness of our arguments. The arguments stood or fell on their own merit. In this particular case, a subsequent mathematical proof confirmed my intuition.

November 20 [NOV 22 ?]

Dear Walter,
"I love Jehovah, because he heareth
My voice and my supplications.
Because he hath inclined his ear unto me.
Therefore will I call upon Him as long as I live." Psalm
116:1,2.

Isn't it wonderful that we can call upon God at all times? Oh,
that I would use this wonderful gift more. It seems as though God
is so near that I can whisper into His ear at times. I am so happy
that He does not tire of me but continues to shower blessings upon
me.

Walter, I am sorry that I have not been able to answer your
letter sooner. There was one question which you asked which I was
unable to answer until tonight. You asked about spending
Christmas holidays with us in Clarissa. Well, I wrote home to find
out if it was all right with the folks. You see, we have such a small
home and a parish worker rooms at my brother's place. I was afraid
it would be so crowded that you maybe wouldn't enjoy it and the
folks would think it wise to have your room some other place. I
received a letter this evening telling that I could invite you as the
parish worker is not to be there during Christmas. Walter, I hope
that you will be able to come and I hope you will enjoy your visit
in Minnesota.

Walter, I am so happy about getting the chance to practice on the accompaniment to Handel's oratorio, "The Messiah." The community chorus of Washburn renders this oratorio each Christmas. I am to play the accompaniment. The two glee clubs are to sing in the chorus.

It is health building to take physical exercises and soul strengthening to meditate on God's word each morning before starting the day's work. I am sure that God will richly bless you and you will be better able to serve Him. That is the only reason that God has put us here on earth – to bring us nearer to Him and to bring others to Him. I wish that I could serve Him more.

May God bless and keep you and your dear ones until He comes for to take you unto Himself in glory.

Sincerely,

Margaret.

"It is health building to take physical exercises" sounds like taking medicine. It was Dad's "fit and supple" ideal that took seed my freshman year at Colorado State University. For a few dollars I purchased a circular rope with an instruction book of isometric exercises; however, lacking a clear measure of progress, I soon discarded the rope.

I purchased a set of exercise springs my sophomore year. Progress, measured by increasing the number of repetitions or attaching an additional spring between the handles, was eventually outweighed by snagged hairs and overstretched springs.

I invested in a set of barbells my senior year. By year's end, my modest progress and declining expectations ceased compensating for the time, effort, and inconvenience.

Interest revived in graduate school when I ran across a booklet on aerobic exercises put out by the Royal Canadian Police. No ropes, no springs, no barbells; only the physical movement of my body. Although mirrors failed to offer any rewards, I felt more limber and energetic. I advanced a few levels before the additional time and effort again won out — but not entirely. I still enjoyed stretching back and then bending forward to touch my toes ten times each morning when I got up. The ritual left me limber and refreshed and took little time and effort. Later, I finally realized that I had found at least one rejuvenating exercise that I could do the rest my life.

Sunday in the late afternoon.

I just returned from Messiah rehearsal. The Girls' Glee Club came to practice nearly one hundred percent. About one-half of my boys came. The boys are to have a special practice this week. I do hope they will be willing to come. Some of the boys have some fine voices. Will you pray that they will come, if it is His will?

We had a delicious turkey dinner down at the hotel this noon. Last night the Norwegian Lutheran Ladies Aid served a "lutefisk and lefsa" supper. They took in some over $90.

Margaret

Scandinavians in America are a select group that can turn lutefisk dinners into Christmas fund-raisers. The mysterious appeal of this preparation is well captured in Wikipedia:

> Lutefisk is... a traditional dish . . . gelatinous . . . extremely strong, pungent odor . . . made from dried whitefish . . . soaked in . . . cold water and lye . . . two days . . . producing a jelly-like consistency . . . therefore caustic . . . to make the fish edible . . . another four to six days of soaking in cold water . . . must therefore be cooked carefully so that it does not fall into pieces.

This morning I was at the Bible class. He, the minister, taught the class showing the Kingdom of Grace and of Evil. Next Sunday I hope to take notes on the discussion. I hope your pupils were drawn nearer to Him because of their being in your class.

Margaret

I just returned from playing for one of the high school girls while she sang a solo at . . . the Eproth League and then the Luther League. At the Luther League we had a question box. Such topics as: How may I know I am a Christian? What can our League do to stop the bridge playing fad in Washburn? and finally Can a League member work in the Eproth and his own church? The topics were well discussed. Rev. Berg added remarks after the members had finished all discussion and I went away feeling that I as a Lutheran cannot attend and worship in a reformed church when there are services at the same time in the Lutheran Church. I hope I haven't started the high school pupils' going to the Methodist League when they belong to the Lutheran Church. I wonder if I am responsible? I need to bring it to God in prayer. I have been a stumbling block, if I have. I attended the Methodist Church services in the evening as the Lutheran Church had no services except for Luther League and that only for high school pupils. Now I see it all in a different light and I plan to attend Luther League every Sunday night that the League has charge and try to be of service to the members and especially to worship God. Oh that I were more surrendered to Christ and His Church.

There is no difference so small that a spirit of separation cannot insert a wedge. I encountered one such puzzling chink while attending a joint meeting of Luther Leagues of

65

the Augustana Lutheran and Missouri Lutheran Synods. We enjoyed mixing together once the comfortable cliques that naturally exist among shy teenagers broke up—until the issue of Sunday's joint communion service arose. Some of us had evidently been taught that Lutherans from different synods should not sit at the same table when celebrating the communion that, ironically, was instituted by a Jewish rabbi to help his followers become one in spirit.

Nov. 25 [NOV 25 10 PM]

Dear Margaret:

Thou art my God, and I will give thanks unto thee;

Thou art my God, I will exalt thee.

Oh give thanks unto Jehovah for he is good;

For his loving kindness endureth forever. Psalm 118; 28,29.

Thanks be to God for his unspeakable gift. 2 Cor. 9; 15.

Many people are this day celebrating a day; set aside by our president, after a custom established by our forefathers many years ago. To celebrate; it is such a general word and to my mind it brings a picture of hilarity and wantonness. So it is, with many; it means excessive eating and especially drinking of alcoholic liquors. I dread to pick up the papers tomorrow, for I know what the headlines will contain, a statement of holiday deaths with many more permanently injured.

Thanks be to God for his unspeakable gift. I am glad that I could enjoy eating turkey and fixins with many of the relatives; there is much fine fellowship there and much common ground. But today I thank a loving God for a gift, which enables me to walk through every day in the year; fearing nothing except such a great giver.

Margaret; I was so glad to see and read, that you too feel that God is very near to you. It does seem that you could grasp his hand; does it not? Then you can pour out all your thots to him,

67

and experience the wonderful joy and blessing of his fellowship. That is true communion with God and our prayers should be such. I am sorry that thru my many sins I do not always feel so near to Him but I thank him for standing by my side when I can no longer carry the load. . . .

Margaret, I am glad that you have some time for your music. You love it and God uses it so much in the furtherance of His Kingdom. I have heard some who are very skeptical Christians, if they are such at all, sing a song like; "The Living God". Their faces would glow as they sang it and I am sure it was an influence for the better in them.

Margaret I can stay in town very nicely. I would not want to be too much an inconvenience. I thank you for your effort and work in writing home just to find a place for me. Thank you again. I am sure I will enjoy my visit very much. I can almost visualize going to the wonderful "Julotta" service in the crisp Minnesota air. Perhaps you will sing then, or some time while I am there. I enjoy hearing you very much. I think that the first time I noticed Margaret Leaf in more than just a passing way, was when she sang one of our hymns, in church one Sunday morning. I've forgotten the name of the hymn but not the way you put your heart in it.

And now may God keep you and bless you and use you, to the end that someday all may live in Christ Jesus.

Walter

Julotta, a Christmas church service timed to end when the sun rose, was another Swedish tradition I could not justify. We had to get up early to dress and to drive to church in time for the service, a less onerous constraint in Sweden with their long winter nights.

Hearing Mom sing, on the other hand, was pure joy. When she hung clothes underneath a bright blue Colorado sky, she often vocalized in clear, ringing tones: up the scale, "Do re mi fa so la ti do;" down the scale, "Do ti la so fa me re do." After repeating this sequence a few times, she often began another exercise. Starting on the fifth of a major chord, she went up to the eighth, and back down to the fifth, third, and base note singing, "To Thee-ee we sing." Starting again on the fifth with "To," she stayed there and soundly emphasized each syllable of "Thee we si-" before descending to the base of the octave with "ing." This exercise was repeated starting a half step higher until she reached the limit of her comfortable range.

Sometimes I jumped from behind a large sheet she was hanging on the clothesline and surprised her with a hug. She would hug me back and say, "Oh, I'm so happy" or "Isn't God great?" or "Isn't it a beautiful day?"

Another vocal exercise possibly affected me in a much more subtle manner. She enjoyed trilling the words "Willie, Willie, Willie, Willie, Willie" ascending and descending along the three notes of major chord. I thought the exercise was meant to improve rapid pronunciation. Later it dawned on me she had been unconsciously singing "Willey," my wife's maiden name.

As Walter contemplated his trip north, Margaret initiated a conversational thread on a social activity that would confound her prayers.

November 27 [NOV 29 7 – AM]

Dear Walter,

We had "Messiah" practice this afternoon. There were quite a number to the rehearsal; however, there weren't many of the town's men. Mrs. Mann feels discouraged that they don't take more interest. The music is difficult and there are so many things to do so I expect that accounts for their lack of interest.

I haven't heard about the book by Dale Carnegie, which you mentioned. It is difficult for me to get a hold of the most recent books as I seldom get to the libraries or book stores that carry the most recent books. If it wouldn't be too much bother, I would like to read your copy.

The meals served to us teachers at the hotel are very bountiful. This noon we were served goose with all of the trimmings that go with such a dinner. We had been served "lutefisk" twice. One of the teachers just can't stand the odor from that fish so he has to eat the other kinds of meat. There are certain kinds of food that I can't like to eat so I don't blame him. As a result from these delicious meals I have been gaining in weight. Now I weigh 132 lbs. I guess I'll keep it up for a while, as later in the year, when work piles up, I usually lose my appetite and then I will need some reserve strength.

At League tonight the question of school proms came up. I wish that Ione Eitemiller could have been here as I know that she could have told us many things which would have helped in the discussion. Walter, I can't understand why people can't be interested in other things than cards, dances, and movies. There are so many things that I would enjoy doing, if I only had the leisure time in which to do them.

Did you read about Rev. Eric Hedeen's sudden death? One year while at college about six of us students spent Thanksgiving Day in Topeka in his parsonage. . . . It certainly isn't safe to ride on the highways nowadays when men drive while they are intoxicated. May the Protector ever protect His own.

Thanks for remembering me at the throne of Grace and may He ever be your all in all.

Margaret

December 4 [DEC 6 3 – PM]

Dear Walter,

This is Saturday and I have finished grading a set of test papers and letters of apology and of condolence. This afternoon I plan to prepare my coming week's assignments in Merchant of Venice for English I class.

I surely enjoy "Juiotta" services. My brother usually asks me to sing sometime during Christmas. I am glad that you enjoyed hearing me sing.

Yesterday the pupils were excused to see the movie "The Road Back" by Erich Remarque, a German novelist. Once while in college, I heard Remarque lecture. My father gave the book "All Quiet on the Western Front" to Bernard. This "The Road Back" is a sequel to "All Quiet on the Western Front." I saw the movie last Friday also. It surely pictures war as my brother would describe it. He didn't want to talk about it at all as it was so gruesome. I wish that greed and hatred were not in the human heart. Maybe then, however, we wouldn't long so for heaven. I am thankful that my two brothers came home safely and soundly.

This coming Tuesday the P.T.A. meeting is to be held. The mixed chorus is to sing "Glory to God" and the boys glee club "Why Do the Nations Rage?" from the Messiah. . . . I am to direct the community singing of Christmas carols. Will you please remember this in prayer? I wanted to write this letter sooner so

that you would get this in time on Tuesday but now it is too late.
The train just came thru.

Is your car running just as well as it did last summer? I
imagine you think quite a lot of it since it is so faithful. If I
remember rightly you thought it climbed up Look-Out Mountain
very well. I wish that we could have been up there a little longer
and a little earlier. There was so much to see that was interesting,
educational, and beautiful. Had it been clearer and had the sun
shone it would have been fun to look thru one of those large
telescopes. When you went to visit those people up in Poudre
Canyon did you bring your telescope along?

On a little pamphlet [Rev Berg] gave us . . . it mentions if one
reads three chapters every week and five on Sunday one can read
the Bible in its entirety in one year. I plan to start reading the
Bible thru but I hope to read more chapters per day.

Well, soon Christmas is here and I hope that you come to
Minnesota. I haven't been home for a long time so I can hardly
wait to see the folks. May God bless and keep you in His grace and
peace.

Yours in Christ,
Margaret.

Our family gathered together each night after dinner to
read Egermeir's Bible Story Book. One of us read a chapter

and another prayed. We said the Lord's Prayer together and sang a hymn.

We read the complete book two or three times. The stories and the pictures became a part of me, but they were shortened versions of the real thing. The real thing was described in much smaller print in the Bible.

Somewhere around my tenth birthday, Mom offered me five dollars if I would read the Bible from beginning to end. I jumped at the chance. Five dollars was roughly equivalent to a year's discretionary money. I dutifully read two pages a night. Two years later I collected my five dollars. Mom repeated her offer; I read through the Bible a second time.

The effect on my life was profound. You don't read through the Bible at that young age without coming away with an awe of God and a love for Jesus, not if you believe there is something which we address as God and the nature and character of that something is being faithfully described in the Bible.

Some nagging questions began forming on my second time through. Why didn't miracles similar to the ones in the Bible happen today? How could so many people in the Bible see those miracles and still not believe in God? Exactly what happened when God spoke to Moses from a burning bush or when Jesus spoke to Saul on his way to Damascus? Where was God? How could God allow suffering and wipe out whole cities with his command? The fact that God was aware of my thoughts raised further questions: What is mind and how is mind tied up with God?

Although I would not read through the Bible again for many years, the questions occasionally bubbled up through crevices and cracks in my metaphoric grounding and subsided when answers were not forthcoming.

A GLIMPSE BACK

November 11. Walter and Margaret were concerned about the prospect of war. What world issues concern you? Where do you see your responsibility in addressing those issues?

November 20. Margaret described an intimacy with the source of her being as "whispering in His ear." Have you ever felt close to the source of your life? What were those times like and what occasioned them?

December 4. In her reflection on war, Margaret longed for freedom from greed and hatred. When you contemplate world conflict, what do you long for? How is your longing reflected in your view of heaven?

THERE ARE NOT MANY

On December 5 readers of the Greeley Tribune learned that Mrs. Cora Brinkman died in a car accident. Less than a week later they learned that the WPA (Works Progress Administration) planned to hire 350,000 more workers.

Dec. 5 [DEC 8 10 PM]

Dear Margaret:

Now thank we all our God with hearts and hands and voices.

Margaret; we should be thankful, to such a patient, kind and loving God; With all the faculties of both mind and body. I often wonder at His loving kindness; at his patience even though I sin so often. He is truly a glorious friend and righteous Father.

I am reminded of all this as I behold the glorious view from my window at Home. The sun is shining in its fullest brilliance with a few white fleecy clouds floating around in the heavens. I can now see the houses and buildings that last summer were hid in the green foliage of the trees around them. Only the skeleton of the tree is now visible. The cattle are resting in perfect contentment, out of the wind, behind a windbreak built of boards, for the purpose of protecting them from the harsh north wind. The wind is very gently stirring thru the dead limbs of the trees, not singing of winter, but merely telling of its near approach. It sings a prophetic song.

I am at home this afternoon because I have quite a few little things to be done. In the first place this has been a busy week, Sunday evening at church, Monday eve, a committee met to order books and awards for the Christmas program, Tues. rifle club, "an old and favorite hobby of mine["], of which I am not sure of God's will, concerning it. Will you pray that His will concerning this may soon be made clear to me. Wed. eve. I stayed at home. Thurs. eve. a joint meeting of the two church boards, Fri. eve. Luther League, Sat eve. nothing and Sun. eve. our League goes to Bethany Denver.

Dad's being a member of a rifle club must have been God's will. I occasionally went to watch. The target sheets hung at the ends of rectangular bales of straw aligned at the far end of the high school gymnasium. The contestants lined up at the other end with their twenty-two-caliber target rifles, each with a heavy steel barrel an inch in diameter, a wide positioning strap, and a high-powered scope.

The first time I went along, Dad let me see how the targets at the far end of the gym appeared in the scope. After I lay down in the prone position, he showed me how to steady the rifle with the aid of the positioning strap. Eventually I brought the cross-hairs of the scope to a fitful rest on the BB-sized bull's eye of one of the twelve two-inch targets on the pinned-up sheet.

The contest began with the contestants in the prone position. A starting signal set off a deafening racket. Each shooter fired a single shot at each of the twelve targets on his sheet. When the firing stopped, the sheets were collected and fresh ones pinned on the straw bales. Meanwhile, the contestants assumed the sitting position for the next shooting round. This round was followed by rounds shot from the kneeling and standing positions. Everyone gathered for coffee and doughnuts while the scores were tallied. At the prone and sitting positions, Dad often hit all of the twelve bull's eyes and hit a few in the standing position. He seldom, if ever, came in first among contestants, but usually was among the top third.

There is very little spare time to answer your welcome and refreshing letter, so I will do that now. I am to lecture on the program at League tonight. It is all Swedish, so I have been searching and studying diligently for and upon something to read. You should hear me speåkå svenskä. Nevertheless it is both interesting and instructive.

Rueben and Evodia, have indeed, a very cute little girl in their home, but I have heard no name as yet. They have taken her to the hospital, until her diet becomes regulated. I hope and believe, that she will soon become accustomed to all the changes and can be at home with them. After all it is only a very small mite of life, and is indeed a reflection to His glory, that they soon gain strength and grow into the most wonderful of all machines.

Margaret you mention the discussion concerning proms and other so called social activities. My knowledge is very limited and I do not want to pretend to know a great deal, altho that is one of the chief of my sins. Even so; it seems to me, that the Devil is indeed a great power, and a most subtle enemy. To me it seems, he has two very great weapons; which are within our bodies. The weapons of sloth and lust. To truly know Gods will indeed takes much time, in study of His Word and in prayer. Both are important and go hand in hand, and in most of us is so much sloth, that we say, if we are a little late; Oh well! I'll not read a chap. today and I'll just take a minute to pray, and then we hurry on thinking we will do better tomorrow.

*Margaret; if every Christian would do today, what he planned
to do tomorrow, this would be a wonderful place to live. Then too,
there is much lust in all of us, lust of pride, lust of money, of
security and lust for the gilded happiness offered by the devil. The
continual round of parties, dances, and clubs and theaters. We are
ever going, but where? Margaret; In the Companion for Dec 2; on
the page, "As others See it," there is an article on Virtue, the Sin of
Virtue. I know that as far as I am concerned that I am guilty of this
sin mentioned there. I wonder why people don't see things as I do.
I am glad that I go to church, I am happy that I can pray to God
and come away refreshed. I feel pretty good about teaching S. S.
and sometimes I think, if everyone gave in the same proportion
according to their means financially as I do, that the work of the
church would never suffer. Thru all this comes one thought to my
mind: incessantly, it says: Are you seeking the trouble and inner
peace in the right place. Have you looked upon yourself. Is it
because you are not doing your part that someone else is also
seeking inner peace at the wrong source. Margaret; we should pray
for a spiritual quickening within us. I do not say revival because
the word has been misused so much, but that the Holy Spirit be
sent to dwell in us would indeed be a blessing to us.*

Interestingly, Walter didn't explicitly come out against
dancing. Instead he was more concerned about excessive

pride, the thirst for money, the lure of security, and the glitter of happiness.

My understanding of Dad's approach to moral issues is well reflected in his words "Are you seeking the trouble and inner peace in the right place?" Although I often knew where he stood on a moral issue, he always left me feeling that my stand was ultimately my responsibility. More than once he remarked, "It's not hard to do what is right, once you know in your heart what is right."

Dad seemed to know in his heart where he stood on a moral issue. My heart often struggled with what I would like to do, but my sense of God, and often my timidity, would not let me do.

If every Christian would realize that even though, he read the word some every day and came to God in daily prayer; that he was a vile sinner, "just as Paul did," and would admit to God that; I cannot even come to you, though I want to. Then ask God to so surround me that I cannot get away from you, ask Him to use me in order that others might know, the glorious freedom of being a slave, to do only God's will.

Margaret; I am not sure that you understand all this, which I have written and there is much more of which I have been thinking but it is not clear to me. I asked God to help me and I think it is

His will that I write no more of it now. I hope that it has not harmed you, but rather helped you. For I pray for you. Not just as a girlfriend, but as a true Christian friend to whom and with whom I may discuss, the many problems that arise before us. I pray that our Father may make plain to you, the truth, the way and the light.

Margaret: I am afraid to get down on my knees and confess to God my true nature, I am afraid to walk in the way unflinchingly and unashamed. For if I did the truth would be revealed to me and I would have to go out and work; work; work; until my strength was spent, in order that many souls might know the glorious gospel of Jesus Christ. It may only mean the spare time I have to put on it; besides my task of providing daily bread, but if I would admit it; it would give me much time to work for Him. Nevertheless though I am afraid as yet; yet I pray for the day to come, soon when my first thought shall be for the Kingdom of God. I am asking Him to give me the courage, to help me overcome that fear and to increase my faith so that I may come to Him, dedicate my life and willingly become his instrument to the salvation of many souls.

Why I write to you these things I do not know, but there are not many with whom I can discuss these problems. I thank you for your patient and considerate understanding friendship. Please pray for me. I am convinced that if God will have me at all, it will be on my knees in humble submission to His will.

Now may God's Guardianship be your consolation at all times and ever keep you in Christ Jesus.

Walter

A soul mate—someone with whom you can share your deepest thoughts. What a find!

The wanderings of the mind are puzzling. Margaret expressed a concern with the desirability of high school proms and Walter ended up talking about "the glorious freedom of being a slave, to do only God's will." Here's a take on that enigmatic statement.

The more I am involved in concerns that give joy and meaning to my life, the greater is my sense of freedom in being about what I want. Duty and distractions are also a part of life. They too can be interesting and enjoyable, yet I find that when these things start occupying the bulk of my time, an urging to return to those concerns closer to my heart grows stronger and increasingly insistent. A sense of freedom sweeps over me when I answer the call of my joy. I am its willing slave.

Therein lays a danger. Could you ever be mistaken or misled? Could your involvement in a job or a calling ever reach a point that you found yourself separated from your joy? It would be disappointing to look back on life and wish that you had spent less time at work and more time with your family, to feel that you were so occupied with earning a living that you never took time to enjoy life, or to sense that you never found a way of helping others that brought lasting meaning to your life. Consequently, I often meditate on the question, "Does all sit right with me?"

December 8 [DEC 8 430 PM]

Dear Margaret:

In the 1st Chap. of Ephesians the 9th verse, we find this short statement: "making known unto us the mystery of his will, according to his good pleasure which he purposed in him."

God's will is indeed mysterious unto us. It will indeed be a glorious day when that mystery will be fully revealed unto us.

Day before yesterday I was a pall bearer at Mrs. Cora Brinkman's funeral. "I believe that you visited them at Windsor, Colo. When you were here last summer." It is hard to understand why a young mother should be taken from those, who in our sight need them so much. There was much consolation in the fact that she was ready to go, in order to be with her Heavenly Father. Even so the shadow of that mysterious will often persists in hanging over us.

Then yesterday afternoon a few friends gathered together with Rev. and Mrs. Carlson, While they said farewell to a little stranger so recently taken into their home. It is sad and very hard on both of them. They had much worry, while their little girl was ill and then Mrs. Brinkman's sudden death, was a distinct shock and severe loss to them. Three ministers and Gilbert Satloff were present; Rev. Conrad, Rev. Segerhammer and Rev. Peterson.

Rev. Conrad reminded us of the promise of our Lord; "That is as much as ye did it even unto the least of these; My brethren, ye did it unto me." Matt. 25[,40].

From Heb: 13,2., "Forget not to show love unto strangers for thereby some have entertained angels unawares," comes an admonishing thought to me. In this rapidly moving age, we are prone to forget this admonishment.

The testimony of faith which has been shown by Rev. and Mrs. Carlson is beautiful and edifying, and it is my prayer that the strength of God, which comes from such faith may be theirs during this hour of trial.

The Christmas season is coming on at a great speed, bringing with it, all the hustle and bustle of Christmas shopping. The Shadow of greed and commercialism hangs over it all, but not too heavy, so as to obscure the vision of the true Christmas spirit; the spirit of Love and with it, God's great gift to all mankind.

Do you have snow on the ground in North Dakota? And do you wake up on the cold and crispy morning with the thermometer hovering below the zero mark? We have some snow on the ground, about 4 inches. It fell during the last two days. Last night was the first night the thermometer has registered below zero. It was 5° below last night.

The air seemed so clear, clean and crisp this morning. It was good to expel the old air from your lungs and fill them with the new clean air.

By the way; how many suits of red underwear is it customary to wear while in Minnesota? The old adage; "While in Rome do as the Romans do["] must hold true for Minnesota also. Saturday Dec. 4, Evodia was telling of some temperatures she had seen and experienced while there. I was almost frightened into waiting until July to visit there, but I think I can stand the climate, if all things else work to the end that I might visit with you.

I must go up to my place to do some work; so now may God's Grace, keep you always in Christ Jesus.

Walter

The understanding that the universal realm in which we live is ultimately good is buried deep within us. In the first chapter of the Bible we read:

> *In the beginning God created the heavens and the earth . . .*
> *So God created man in his own image . . . And God blessed*
> *them . . . And God saw everything that he had made, and*
> *behold, it was very good.*

However, the word good didn't bubble up as Walter tried to get his mind around the untimely deaths mentioned in his letter. Although he felt some comfort that flowed from his vision of life after death, still "the shadow of that mysterious will" troubled him.

Dec 9 [DEC 14 430 PM]

Dear Margaret:

Let the words of my mouth and the meditation of my heart be acceptable in thy sight, O Jehovah, my rock, and my redeemer.

Margaret; these lines come from the 19th psalm. If you have time, read the whole psalm. It is a treasure, with many truths in it.

Perhaps you remember my saying last summer, that I did not care much to read the psalms. I understand them better now and enjoy reading them. Can it be that God gave them to us, that we might see the example of fellowship, which it is our privilege to have with him our Father in Heaven.

One of my greatest desires is to someday hear the Messiah given. Please find out when it is to be given, at the place you mention. It may be that arrangement could be made so that I might hear it. If money was more plentiful, I would drive my car and it would become more easy to arrange. I should like for you and your mother and also brother and family, to go also.

As it is now, I shall probably come by bus. If so I may have to go, by way of the cities. If possible, I shall get a pass to go to Omaha on a stock train then I will only have to pay fare from Omaha to Minn. One pass is given for each carload of livestock. My stock is not yet fat enough to go but I believe I can get help, to get a pass to Omaha or Chicago.

I neither saw nor read, Remarque's sequel to "All quiet on the Western Front," but I both read and saw the latter. It certainly pictures the horror of War. May God grant us, to be our Ally both in and out of War, especially our continual war against sin.

By the time I came around, movies were broadly accepted by the Greeley community. Dad and Mom took us to see The Living Desert, The Vanishing Prairie, and Martin Luther. My youngest sister, Anna, told me that when she was in the seventh grade Dad and Mom were given their first TV, a used one with a rabbit-ears antenna. She related that they didn't watch much at first, but eventually came to enjoy a number of situation comedies. Mom particularly enjoyed The Flip Wilson Show, but disliked any mimicking of drunken or mentally handicapped behavior. Dad also enjoyed Gunsmoke and later the detective shows Columbo and The Rockford Files.

I can skate, but not very well as I have weak ankles. I used to jump from any haystack or building, I could find and it did not help my ankles any. Nevertheless I enjoy trying to skate and being out in the clean fresh air. I wish I knew how to ski. It seems to me that it would be much fun. You speak of playing volley ball and tennis. I enjoy playing the latter. I wish I had known you played for I should like to have played with you. I have heard that your brother Phillip is a very good player.

I have traded my car for a coupe of a year later model. My car needed paint and some work on it. I thought I was getting a pretty good trade so I went through with it. It is a Chevrolet though.

I have not taken my telescope with me, for some time. Another party has ½ interest in it. We bought it to spot the rifle shots, in the targets at the rifle club. It is necessary to see each shot and you cannot see those small holes at 50 ft. This kind of rifle shooting is very exacting. The bulls eye is about this large O.

I set out to read thru the Bible once, but during the beet season I failed to keep up, so I only got about 1/2 or 2/3 thru the new testament, perhaps a little more. If I remember rightly, I read some into one of the Epistles of John. I have read most of the New Testament more than once, so I feel that I have read thru it. Nevertheless I plan to read thru it, in its consecutive order, this year also. I believe I will get more out of it this time. I plan to read more slowly, carefully and prayerfully.

Many great men have read thru the Bible many times. They know the value of the Wisdom contained therein. The inner peace and quiet which God gives thru the knowledge of His word and Will. We would indeed gain much power if we would diligently seek his will and wisdom in His Word.

By the forepart of this week I shall try to know definitely how all things will go. Then I shall write you and try to set a definite date as to when I shall arrive.

Now may this find you well and always in Christ Jesus.
Walter

I knew Dad had played tennis and baseball when he was younger. Two tennis rackets and two baseball gloves hung on a wall of the staircase leading to the basement of our farmhouse. He had mentioned having played with his sister, my Aunt Irene, but I don't believe he had picked up a tennis racket after I was born.

I started playing tennis in college. One afternoon I walked into a house our family had recently rented. Dad noticed the two tennis rackets I was carrying and asked if he could see them. "Sure."

He mentioned how tennis rackets had changed since he used to play. "Want to hit a few; maybe play a game or two?"

I didn't know what to expect. He was in his early sixties and never played tennis when I was growing up. Would he even be able to return the ball?

The accuracy was no longer there, but the strength and form of his backhand and his ability to curve the ball to the right or to the left when serving was a total surprise. It dawned on me that Dad had enjoyed a leisure and affluence I had not associated with the long hours of farm work.

December 12 [DEC 13 – 7AM]

Dear Walter,

"Call upon me in the day of trouble: I will deliver thee, and thou shalt glorify me." Ps. 50:15.

Thanks for the letters which I received from you this past week. It was sad to hear of the deaths of the baby and of Mrs. Brinkman. It doesn't seem true. God knows what is best for His children so we just leave it all to Him to carry us through. I can just see those two darling children of Brinkman's. Mrs. Brinkman was a consecrated Christian so she is now with her Lord. One of my sisters passed away a short time before Christmas two years ago. I can imagine that the Christmas festivities with Christ are perfect so they are exceedingly joyful. May God give Mr. Brinkman the comfort which He alone can give. Evodia and Reuben would have been so very happy to have the baby with them during the Christmas season but then they have so many little children in the Sunday School upon whom they can shower their love.

Clara, Margaret's sister, died giving birth to a still-born child. More than once Mom related to me that her husband, John Anderson, was unwilling to take Clara to a younger doctor Clara preferred.

My sister Lois said that Clara had trimmed a satin cap in lace for the infant in her womb. Mom had saved the cap. Lois said that when our youngest sister, Anna, was born, Mom was asked to see how that cap would look on Anna's head. Mom wouldn't do it.

We have but one week and a half of school. When Mr. Thorson announced the time of vacation to the pupils I am afraid I was happier than many of the students. We begin our semester reviews after vacation. We have but one week of review and a week for tests at that time. Time moves along rapidly.

The Eng. III class are giving debates this week. They were told to make a list of questions and from the list choose any four. One of the questions which they chose is Resolved: that our high school sponsor a yearly prom. Two of the boys came to me and said they couldn't think of a single way in which a prom would be beneficial. I hope God will speak to them while they are debating so that He can take full control.

I guess you are right concerning one's overlooking a person's own faults and condemning others. I read the article. . . . It might be that He has caused it so that you are to correspond with me so that I may be drawn nearer to Him. I love the Lord with my whole heart but Satan and my flesh creep in and then I must seek the Lord again. I know that you wrote the thoughts concerning yourself and your need of more consecration to help me so I truly thank you. I am so happy that you are living for Him and I want to live closer to Him than I am but I am so gratified that I know Him and am persuaded that He is able to keep me and you unto the day when He comes to claim us for Himself in His heavenly mansions with all His saints. I would never correspond in the way that I do with you if I didn't know that you were a Christian and wanted to draw others to Christ. If I were better able to write for Christ I would so but He has to put the finishing touches: I can't.

The soloist from Bismarck could not come to sing the Messiah when the date was set so the attempt has finally been given up.

May God bless and keep you for Him. I hope to see you soon but, if it's impossible, I know that God doesn't want you to come so it will be all right.

Yours in Christ,

Margaret

P.S. I wonder how the Swedish speaking turned out. I think the Swedish language is beautiful and I especially like the songs. It seems to me the thought is truer, deeper, and [more] expressive than in the English. There are some pupils at school who can speak the German language.

By the time I came along, Swedish services were no longer held at our church. A few of the older members spoke English with a strong Swedish brogue. They especially enjoyed the times Mom and three other choir members sang "Children of Our Heavenly Father" in Swedish.

At home, Swedish was essentially a secret code spoken across the dinner table when Dad and Mom wished to keep shared concerns or observations from our inquisitive ears. I learned a few Swedish words and the names of our favorite Swedish dishes, but lacked the desire to read or speak Swedish. My oldest brother, Paul, who lived a few years in Sweden, said that the Swedish spoken today in America reflects a century-old dialect no longer spoken overseas.

Dec 15 [DEC 19 10 PM]

Dear Margaret:

Oh give thanks unto Jehovah; for he is good; For his loving kindness endureth forever.

Margaret; we have the best snowstorm in several years, to be thankful for, in Colorado. It has changed the picture and also created much extra work. I had planned to write to you some sooner but when it was snowing so hard Monday, I decided to wait a little to see the outcome. A cold wet snow is very hard on livestock so I wish to haul plenty of straw to make them comfortable, and also to make other provisions for them. Even so I cannot say definitely when I will arrive for I plan to go to Denver Monday morning and there, I will try to catch a stock train to St. Paul. I have heard since I last wrote that there is a good possibility of doing so.

If possible, I shall write again and if not; may God watch over you and keep you, always in Christ Jesus, Our Lord.

Walter

December 16 [DEC 17 3–PM]

Dear Walter,

"Blessed be the Lord, who daily beareth our burden,

Even the God who is our salvation." Ps. 68:19.

This verse surely is of strength to me as I go about my work. I am glad that God is not partial to His children but He treats me the same as any one of them. He bears your burdens too. May He ever daily bear them for He is our salvation.

It will be fine if you can get a pass on a stock train that you mentioned. Traveling is expensive but I do enjoy it.

This coming Saturday the boys' and girls' glee clubs are to go Christmas caroling. Will you remember them in prayer? They sing quite well but I need a Higher power to help them to sing as they should.

The Eng. III class are just about thru with debates. The group that is to continue to debate tomorrow because of lack of time to complete two debates during class period[,] asked to have one minute added to their main speeches, as a result, each speaks for three minutes and then, too, they wanted more time on the refutation proper. The pupils seem to enjoy the work. Each time certain pupils are given different parts to play as: one acts as superintendent, three, as judges, two as time keepers, one as teller, six as debaters, and the remaining pupils as the audience. The prom question had as its judges' decision 2-1 in favor of the affirmative that a prom should be sponsored by the class. I was sorry about the outcome but the negative side seemed so weak in their arguments. They weren't persuasive enough. I guess that is the way with most of us we know what is right but do not know how to influence others to see the right in its fullness.

This evening I began to think how sad Reuben and Evodia feel about their losing the baby. Maybe they think God doesn't want them to bring up any children and thus frustrated their plan by taking this one. I wish that they could soon adopt another.

You mentioned about skiing in your letter. My sister Ruth has a pair of skis. She is quite a good skier. I am not very graceful so it is nothing uncommon for me to fall down. I hope you will get the chance to ski. If you bring your camera along I'll take your picture with your skis on. There are those who will lend you skis. I plan to try skiing again because falling down doesn't really hurt one. My ankles are strong enough but the equilibrium is not always up to par while I am on skis.

I wonder if you are a carpenter or not. The table on which I am writing has been gradually coming to pieces while I have been writing this letter. I finally stopped to put one of the legs into its proper position, when a second leg decided to follow the first legs example. I have put both into place but I am barely moving my hand while writing because I fear it will again decide to fall apart.

My English II class is just finishing reading George Eliot's novel, "Silas Marner." That story is very sad. English I class has come to [the] part in Shakespeare's "Merchant of Venice" where Shylock is demanding the pound of flesh. They can't understand how he can be so cruel. Eng. IV class have handed in essays. I haven't graded yet but I plan to wake early and go to school to do that. It is hard for me to grade papers at night so, if God wills it, I hope to be able to return the graded essays tomorrow.

Now I hope that you can make the needed arrangements so that you may be able to make the trip to Minnesota. I'll be looking for you. I do pray that god will guide and protect you on your journey. I am glad that you aren't driving as it seems to ride alone is very hazardous nowadays when drink seems to rule the traffic.

God be with you.

Margaret

We wouldn't have metaphors for inanimate objects if they didn't seem to have a mind of their own. I need only to recall the many times when my wrench slipped on a nut while I was changing parts on a cultivator. When the back of my hand slammed against a sharp corner of a neighboring bar or blade, I often corrected the wrench's ill behavior by instinctively whacking it against the unsuspecting, but nonetheless culpable, steel obstruction. Carrying out this correction was strangely satisfying, and I can vouch that the wrench seldom slipped when reapplied to the obstinate nut. Need I point out that it would have been self-defeating to alter the shape of the causative nut by hitting it with the wrench?

Mom took her metaphors to a more conscious level. When hoeing weeds with us, she often remarked how the devil or Satan was responsible for the weeds and that we had to cut them out by the root or they would grow right back. She would then go after the weeds with renewed vigor. If we noted a camouflaged pig weed she had overlooked in the row she was weeding, she would go back and yank it out by the root while muttering "that old Delilah."

Dec. 20 [DEC 21 830 AM]

Dear Margaret:

Brethren, I count not myself yet to have laid hold: but one thing I do, forgetting the things which are behind, and stretching forward to the things which are before, I press on toward the goal unto the prize of the high calling of God in Christ Jesus. Phil. 3:13-14.

Margaret; there are many verses in the Bible which I love and which help me, including the splendid verse you sent in your last letter. What would we do if he did not bear our burdens? I believe that verse is the answer; to the question: why so many suicides.

Nevertheless there are few verses that I like to read, think of and meditate upon more than this one; that Paul wrote to Philippi. Gods calling in Christ Jesus is indeed high and most worthy of the effort we expend toward it. Let us pray for his strength to help us strive ever toward that calling; so that we may become a mirror of light, unto others, reflecting the love, which he has so graciously given unto us. I too thank God for letting me come to him in prayer, for letting me cast my burdens upon him just as you do. I pray that someday our faith may be increased so that doubt may be banished from us.

Tomorrow morning I will go to Denver. I believe I will get a pass to Austin Minn. If I do I will leave tomorrow eve, "Tues."

and arrive at Austin Wed. eve. I shall send a wire; once I am on
my way in order that you may know definitely, when I will arrive.

Now, may God keep you and bless you in Christ; thru out this
Christmas season and the coming New Year; God willing that we
have another year of Grace.

Yours in Christ,
Walter

Casting off one's burdens is like attempting a backward landing on a trampoline. Many of us have seen the trampoline gently catch and lift back up those who trust its rhythm. I'm told you simply let go and let the trampoline do the work. In my few attempts at landing on my back, I inevitably twisted slightly to see that the landing would be OK. The trampoline always responded with an uncompromising jolt.

How does one fall back into the arms of life and let life take over once all that can be done has been done? I cannot say. Yet many are buoyed up in the waves and swells of life. For some the required understanding follows upon an overwhelming difficulty or irreversible tragedy. Others are born trusting.

WESTERN UNION TELEGRAM 832 A December 23

Miss Margaret Leaf, Clarissa, Minn. Arrive at 450. Walter Johnson

A GLIMPSE BACK

*D*ecember 5. In what Walter saw as a "continual round of parties, dances, and clubs and theaters," he felt we were "ever going," but wondered where. Have you ever felt you were doing a lot of going, but were unsure as to where? What circumstances brought that feeling about and what understandings assuaged the feeling?

December 8. Walter mentioned "the true Christmas spirit" and the "spirit of love." Have you ever been caught up in the "spirit of a holiday gathering?" Must spirits be real for that to happen, or can it happen simply because one believes in spirits or likes to act as if they exist?

December 9. Walter speaks of an "inner peace and quiet" that comes through knowledge of "[God's] word and Will." What understandings bring an inner peace to you?

December 12. If you were in Margaret's English III class today or in a discussion group, what questions would you like debated?

December 20. Walter enjoyed meditating on the notion of a high calling. In what endeavors have people found a high calling? Is there a way that being a waitress or a garbage collector can be viewed as high endeavor? What high endeavor is "calling" you? How will you respond?

THIS PAST CHRISTMAS

While Margaret was on vacation, readers of the Washburn Leader learned that Uncle Sam promised a "billion dollar bounty" to farmers, that America held the key to the "next world war or peace," and that General Craig wanted to increase the reserve army. After Margaret's return, the Washburn Leader announced an upcoming President's Ball. While Walter was on vacation, readers of the Greeley Tribune learned that Roosevelt wanted 800 million for building the navy and that 44,272 Coloradoans said they were idle. The day Walter's next letter was posted, heifers sold for $8.

Jan. 7 [JAN 8 430 PM, 1938]

Dear Margaret:

"Jehovah is merciful and gracious, Slow to anger, and abundant in loving kindness. Psalm, 103:8.

Margaret; we do certainly have a kind and loving God, who extends to us such an abundance of unmerited mercy.

As I look back upon this last Christmas season, I realize that there is no way of measuring, the love, that God has for us; His Children. How thankful I am to Him; for leading me to you, and for your love and understanding fellowship. . . . To have been with you and prayed with you, has helped me and made it easier to come to Him in prayer and fellowship.

I got home Thurs. morning about 10:30 o'clock. I had a safe and pleasant journey home.

I am tired tonight, because I went to the business meeting at church last night and since I got very little sleep, the two nights I was on the bus and train I am very sleepy. It was 11:30 before we got home from the business meeting. By the way I have another good reason for coming for you as soon as possible, I was elected S. S. Supt. last night and I need some help to pick out songs and in other matters.

Saturday noon.

I gave up writing last night, for I could no longer keep awake. I just returned from my place, where I have been looking after a few things.

I had two invitations to go skating since I came home, one last night and one a week from Sunday. Although my back is improving, I am not taking any more chances of taking a fall until I am entirely well. If I go at all I will tend the fire and cook the coffee.

I have received some good news also. S. S. Brown, my landlord, has a married son, who has a cook stove and heater stored in my house, also a small table, good enough to serve the purpose. I can use these so it will save me quite a bit now and it will also make it possible for you to choose these appliances when you get here.

I was quite encouraged by the market reports, I heard yesterday, at the farmers institute, in Greeley. It is a three day meeting, for Weld County farmers. They have a large seed exhibit and a full program, of competent speakers on the various problems, which confront the farmer. . . . I forgot a shirt at Clarissa with your mother. I am going to write to her, thanking her for the breakfast and many kindnesses. I left in such a hurry.

Yours in Christ,

Walter

Let's speculate on some of the facts that might underlie Walter's thankfulness for Margaret's walking into his life. Walter, as a leader of a youth group, was personable and open to meeting people. He had met any number of eligible women in high school, in church, in youth rallies, and in stores and other businesses. None of those encounters were mutually appealing. By the same token, Margaret had met many eligible men in high school, college, youth groups, and teaching. None of those encounters was mutually appealing. Experience and truth merged when Walter wrote, in his December 5 letter, "There are not many with whom I can discuss these problems," for neither Walter nor Margaret shaped their unique attraction for each other. They simply grew up following their joys in life.

Moreover, they played little if any role in initiating the circumstances. Walter's church needed a new pastor. A brother-in-law of Margaret's accepted the call. Although Margaret had the interest, time, and means to leave her home in Minnesota to visit her sister in Colorado, she has not mentioned any hope she may, thereby, have had in meeting someone like Walter.

For Walter, such arguments may have been only fuzzy and evanescent mental flashings. All that we really know is that Walter felt loved and thankful that Margaret walked into his life — and 'Luck' was not the metaphoric word that came to mind.

Jan. 10 [JAN 10 430 PM]

Dearest Margaret:

And whatsoever ye shall ask in my name, that will I do, that the Father may be glorified in the Son.

If ye shall ask anything in my name, that will I do. John 14:13-14.

My prayer shall always be, that someday God will make us conscious, of the richness of these promises. We would certainly not know many moments of anxiety, if we had the faith to cast ourselves, upon his rich promises.

Now Margaret; before I write more, I want to say that, I love you and pray for you always. Not just once or twice a day but there is always a prayer in my heart for you. I will pray for you in your work, play and all your walk of life. I do know that God gives us strength, to bear all things. In fact that is all that keeps my spirit up, now that you are not near.

I had planned to take a few pictures today but the sun is not shinning so I will wait until tomorrow. I have had quite a cold since I came home, so mother advised me to wait and have my picture taken, until my eyes are brighter. Even the best will not be much so I thought it good advice.

I really must go to do some work now, but I just had to write to you. I was so busy during the weekend, that I could hardly write, yet I am ashamed. I shall try to write and do better; but if you are very busy, you need not write but once a week, for I want you to get some rest each night.

Now may God keep you and bless you through each day.

Yours in Christ,

Walter

January 11 [JAN 12 3 – PM]

Dear Walter,

"If ye walk in my statutes, and keep my commandments, and do them; then I will give you rains in their season, and the land shall yield its increase, and the trees in the field shall yield their fruit." Leviticus 26:3,4

Isn't this a wonderful promise to farmers? The people around here seem to be happy because we are having more moisture. It is warm out even though snowflakes fall. It is fine that so much snow has fallen in Colorado.

Thanks for the letter which you sent. I have been wishing you were around but then I know that you sometimes think of me and I am sure that you are praying for me and so I get happy and go to work. Walter, I am so happy to think that someday I am going to live with you. May I be the kind of person that God wants you to have thru life.

I am sure that you enjoyed your trip. Miss Alexander and Miss Kellam were on the same train as I part of the way so I had friends to converse with. I stayed in Bismarck overnight. The next day I got a permanent. Just as I was leaving the hotel to meet Gladys Schultz's sister, who is a stenographer at the capital building, I met a family from Washburn. They said I could go back with them. Janice Hill, their adopted daughter, and I visited at the capital and went thru the many rooms of the Memorial Building.

We reached home at six o'clock p.m. I was supposed to have ridden back with Ed Skalley but I mentioned to him that I had another ride. Ed is the boyfriend of Ruth Schneider, the second grade teacher. The next day I learned that they didn't reach home until the wee hours of the morning. God knows what we need and he knew I should get to Washburn earlier.

It's strange Walter, but people are beginning to say that I have started to use cosmetics such as rouge etc. I guess God realized that I needed some color to my cheeks so He has given me some extra since Christmas.

The book by Carnegie is very interesting. This writer is giving a lecture every Tuesday evening at 9:45 over N.B.C. We planned to listen in but didn't succeed very well. . . .

Last Sunday evening I gave a talk on "Conscience" at Luther League. It went alright but I talked too long, I think. . . . The leaguers surely laughed when I told about my breaking a window once of a store in Tennessee Ridge. . . . My conscience hurt me a great deal about breaking the window but after I had told my father about it he forgave me and I felt at ease. I believe that is the way God will always quiet our consciences and give us inner peace

I just wish that I could come and spend some time with you. I believe your coffee would taste good but I would prefer drinking good milk. I know that you would have a good fire in the heater so that we would keep warm. Then we could kneel together in prayer and read in the Bible and sing together. Would I enjoy the

evening? I should say so. May God bless and protect you also until
we meet and then forever be with you first until we have journeyed
thru life together and later when He has finally taken you to
Himself in the heavenly mansions.

I love you, Walter.

Margaret

I have never heard of a farmers' institute before. I asked Helen
about it and she hadn't either.

When Margaret spoke of her conscience, I thought back
on my early sense of God. At all moments, God knew my
thoughts and actions. Even so, I often said and did wrongful
things. Those wrongful things troubled me; God was always
there. Peace did not come to my heart until I sought God's
forgiveness. Amending the other relationships harmed by
my thoughts and actions followed quite naturally.

Who knows all of the ways peace with our past can
come? A longtime friend related how his life changed one
night as he contemplated the consequences of his
alcoholism. He was walking along a shore on Lake Michigan
peering into a bleak future, unsure of his desire to return to
his wife and job. When he stopped and happened to look

back, a stiff wind was erasing his tracks. In that wind he saw his past being swept clean.

What my friend saw freed him to start a new life. He went back home to his wife. After considerable discussion, he quit his job. He stopped drinking and returned to graduate school. Two years later we met at his pharmaceutical research lab at, what was then, The Upjohn Company.

As Margaret's letter heads south, Walter begins a third letter starting with "My Dear Margaret," after what must have been a number of disappointing walks to the mailbox.

Jan. 13 [JAN ? 430 PM]

My Dear Margaret:

In all thy ways acknowledge him, and he will direct thy paths. Prov. 3:6

I have been reading quite a bit in the book, that you gave me. I have learned quite a bit about prayer from it, although I do not agree with all of it. Perhaps; that is because my experience is not great enough or old enough yet. But one thing I have read and agree with, that is; that we have to become so humble and helpless, that, we cast ourselves upon Jesus, without any reservation whatsoever. Then we will pray as the publican did and as Mary the mother of Jesus did, when the wine was gone at the marriage feast at Cana. Hallisby points out, in his book that Mary had a problem upon her mind. But she knows where to go with it and she goes there directly and presents it, to Jesus in the most simple language possible. Then she leaves it all to him knowing that he will and can help.

Letting go of your "what ifs" and "buts" so that you can freely attend to things you can do something about — well, that's the trampoline problem of landing on your back. Walter wants to fall back "upon Jesus, without any reservation whatsoever . . . knowing that he will and can help."

The Bible tells us that the starry heavens, the seas, the plants and animals, and even humankind were made good — not perfect, no two minds could ever fully agree on that, but good. Science reveals entities ranging from subatomic particles to huge galaxies and uncovers staggering coordination at all levels along the way. What more do we need to know in order to trust that the universal realm in which we abide will buoy us up? It all depends on the understandings that guide what we see and experience in our world.

Now Margaret Dear; it is a long way to N. D. and I cannot see you often, as some young couples have the privilege of doing. That would surely be a privilege, then I could tell you that I do love you and pray for you. Now I must hope that these words convey my meaning for though I cannot pray with you, I can and do pray for you, and these ten days which have gone since I saw you last, are even greater proof, of what you mean to me. Today I wished that you might be here with me; over the radio came announcements of the National Western Stock Show at Denver, and I thot that it would be fun, if we might go. There is much fine stock to see, also a fine rodeo and fancy horse show and then it is always interesting to go thru the huge meat packing plants. Since my bank balance is so slim, I shall stay at home and work.

I plan if I have time Sunday afternoon to visit the old ladies in the Poudre Canyon. I wish that you could come along then for the mountains. must be beautiful with a new blanket of snow upon them.

We had some new snow day before yesterday. In fact it was quite a blizzard. I went out to see how my horses were faring and I froze several spots on my face although I only walked a little over a mile. It was not very cold, "about 20° above zero" but there was a heavy wind with it. . . . With my frozen cheeks, I would appear to have the mumps so I must wait a little to have my picture taken.

Today it was very pleasant to be out working. The thermometer registered 60° in the sun this noon. I hauled hay and straw today. Tomorrow I must take a load of grain to town, to have it rolled for the cattle. I suppose that sounds strange to you, but when you come out here I will show you (stopped to fill my pen) what it is all about. I'll even show you how to pitch hay, milk cows and anything else that you wish. I'll also promise to help wash the dishes, but I guess I'll have to let you do the knitting for our family because I did not seem very handy at it. How are you coming with the bed sox? Have you finished yet? Perhaps you have been too busy, with semester examinations.

Do you have time to see some of the beautiful sunsets which you spoke of or are you working quite hard now? We have had

some beautiful sunsets and tonight is a beautiful moonlight night,
with millions of stars in the sky. . . . I was glad last summer, when
I found that you loved the birds and the flowers, in fact nearly
everything in nature except snakes.

I still have some recollections of the skiing trip and I do not
mean the plate, that Harold gave us either. They are diminishing
but not entirely forgotten. [Dad would often attribute his later
back problems to a severe fall he took when another skier slid over
the toes of his skis.]

Now may god Bless you and keep you, always; in our Lord
and Savior; Christ Jesus.

Yours in Christ,
Walter

Like all good partnerships, marriage is founded on trust
and respect, mutually helpful roles, and clear expectations.
Walter and Margaret's mutual respect was evident in their
opening letters. Now comes the more difficult part of
building trust, establishing complementary roles, and setting
up clear expectations. Walter saw how Margaret could help
with his chores. He promised to help her with the dishes.

January 16 [JAN 17 3 – PM]

Dear Walter,

You mentioned that you came home with a cold, well, so did I. John said I gave you my cold. I'm sorry. I'm sure that your mother will take good care of you so that you will soon be over it. Last night Ruth and Helen decided that I had to get to bed to get rid of my cold. They were over to Thorson's but they called up at nine o'clock to tell me to get to bed. I decided it would be best for me to obey orders so off I went. They came home about 11:45 and hurriedly took matters in their own hands. Ruth rubbed my chest with musterole and Helen reheated lemonade that they had prepared for me at Thorsons. I drank two cups of hot lemonade. They told me that I couldn't leave the house all day Sunday. I feel pretty good this afternoon. They have consented to my sitting up in bed to write this letter.

Mrs. Thorson came to visit me. She said that I had to promise to not grade but throw away not ½ but ¾ of my papers. She made me promise. . . . Oh how I wanted to tell her about you but I want to wait a little longer.

There was a bridge party last night. Three of us teachers who do not play were not invited. Those three were Ruth, Helen, and I. Dorothy said when she started to play she got such a terrible headache and her whole body began to ache. This morning she said she just felt like going to Sunday School even though she still had a sick feeling. I am sure there were others who felt all tired out this morning. I am glad that I wasn't asked.

Yesterday I mended that brown skirt that you noticed needed some needle work done on it. Miss Foster sees to it that I learn how[.] I may use her portable electric Singer sewing machine anytime I wish. . . . I, also, get lonesome. I don't know just why it is but I guess God made it that way. I would even like to comb your hair right now. I guess I am writing this way because I am not feeling so well and all the future looks so bright. You can burn this letter if you like.

This coming semester I am to teach the same subjects but I only reverse the order in teaching literature to Eng. III and IV students and grammar to Eng. II and I. This will be much easier. I love my pupils so I am looking forward to it. We teachers know one another better now. Johnnie and "Tick" every so often tell me if I misstep in anyway that they think shouldn't be they are going to write to Walt in Colorado so that you can know all that is going on. We have a lot of fun around the table. It seems they have ceased telling those dirty stories that to me seemed uncalled for.

I have told Helen of our engagement. Right away she said she had better get her sewing machine to sing away. She wants to sew the wedding dress. I don't plan to tell anyone else until they see the ring but I get so happy about it all so it might run over and then they'll find out.

How are you feeling after your fall? I wish it hadn't have happened. I wonder how the picture will turn out. John planned to snap us just as you were to leave but then you know what a rush there was so he hurriedly put away the camera.

I hope that you enjoyed being Sunday S. Superintendent this morning but I am just wondering about your class of boys. Who has them?

Now may God bless and keep you ever as His own and may I never be a stumbling block for you in your work in His Kingdom.

Yours in Christ,

Margaret

Even though Margaret disliked playing bridge, it is not easy to take Margaret at her word that she liked being left out when she felt lonesome. Were her colleagues uncomfortable playing bridge when she was around? Was she no longer a part of their group? On the other hand, two of her friends were also excluded and, of course, Walter would have a sympathetic ear and encouraging voice. Still, not being invited could set disconcerting refrains at work in her mind.

Jan. 16 [JAN 18 43C PM]

My Dear Margaret:

Ye have not, because ye ask not. Ye ask, and receive not, because ye ask amiss, that ye may spend it in your pleasures. James 4:2-3

My dear Margaret; I certainly did enjoy your letter. I thank you so much for it. You know Margaret; I must confess, that I can hardly believe that God has directed me, to such a friend as you. One to whom I can write and talk to about spiritual things. One who talks with our dear Lord and God and loves to talk about Him to others. The great answers to prayer and the wonderful blessings which are mine during the past year are almost too much for me to understand. I do thank God; a great deal, but not enough for leading me to you.

I am going to teach my S. S. Class, even though I am supt. I plan to get an asst. to take care of the opening and closing order of the S. S.. This will give me time to teach my class which I do not want to drop. Margaret pray that I may be used to guide these young men aright; even to Jesus the dearest friend we will ever have. Pray also; that pride and vanity may not get a hold on me, but that all may be done for His sake and in His name.

I am sending some pictures and a stock report. It comes from Omaha and since it is the first optimistic report, which we have received for some time, I thought I should send it to you. Perhaps God wants to encourage us. Nevertheless His will be done.

These pictures were taken in the afternoon and fortunately are pretty good. I shall number them and try to explain them in such a way as to give you some understanding of what our future house will be like.

As I took pictures 1 & 2 I stood next to the road in the west entrance of the driveway. . . . In 1. you get a good view of the snow covered yard which is quite large. . . . In 2 you see the entrance to the potato dugout, (made with dirt and straw, where we store potatoes all winter. They do not freeze either) my car and the hired man.

The dugout at our farm was a covered, roughly six-foot-deep rectangular pit with an earthen floor and slightly higher cement walls. The sides of its gabled roof were composed of parallel pine poles anchored to the side walls. The poles were covered by a wire netting, on top of which lay a thick deck of straw capped with several inches of dirt that sloped gently to the ground.

A loaded farm truck could pass through the ten-foot-long entrance enclosed by a pair of heavy doors at both ends. After the second doorway the ground dipped into a cavernous interior with three corridors. The central corridor was lined by two rows of vertical pine posts, paired off with heavy cross timbers at the top. Tractors and machinery could be driven between adjacent posts lining the side corridors and parked in the empty spaces not filled with potatoes.

The dense, dark and silent cavern never froze in winter and stayed cool in summer. The dugout was often filled with thick, slightly sweet, yet pungent aromas of earth and potatoes, especially when last year's leftovers were shriveling up in damp corners as they fed long, pale and stringy, shoots seeking whatever light strayed in.

In 3. (which is taken facing S.E.) you see the entrance to the basement which is almost full and very nice, also the chicken house and just in front of it the well and pump house. I mentioned to you that there is warm and cold water in the house but no other modern features such as a bathroom etc. (It is all electrified tho). Therefore to the right is an outdoor toilet. All the ground between the driveway and the fence which you see running directly behind the toilet, is planted in many kinds of flowers and it is truly beautiful.

I cannot do justice with word or picture to the many beautiful plants and flowers around their house (to the right in no 6) . . . I will say this that though Mr. Brown is an atheist and drinks more than any man I know, yet he and the whole family (Mrs & 1

daughter about 40 years of age at home) are fine people. They will
do almost anything for me, in fact they are almost a 2nd home to
me. He knows I will not drink and never asks me anymore, in fact I
know he respects me more for it. I will admit that it is tiresome to
listen to the same old story time & time again when he is under the
weather and wants to talk, but I avoid being around him if
possible.

I am sorting potatoes now and it is a lonely job, to stand there
by yourself. But I think often of you and it spurs me on, knowing
that next year, I can come in and talk to Margaret, maybe you will
cook a cup of coffee for me and dry a rusk.

I expect Walter could have walked around all day by
himself and not felt lonely. Not so in a dugout, where he
probably flicked on a small lightbulb and started sorting
potatoes.

Sorting potatoes was a monotonous task. A forkful of
potatoes was scooped into the top of the sorter. The desired
ones were guided to the "seed" side; the others were pushed
to the "market" side. The sorted potatoes fell into separate
gunny sacks hanging on hooks. At first one noted the
sounds of the sorter jiggling the potatoes rolling down the
sorting belt. Once those sounds morphed into a gentle
background noise, the mind naturally wandered.

I must go now, so I wish Gods rich blessing upon you and may He keep you always in His Grace.

Be always of Good Cheer for I pray for you always and love you more each day.

Yours in Christ,

Walter

Walter's acceptance of Mr. Brown may reflect his upbringing. Dad's father, Claus Arvid Johnson (Farfar, in Swedish), was a founding member of the Lutheran church and a board member of Lone Tree School, the grade school Dad attended. I later learned that Farfar enjoyed having a beer with friends and on rare occasions drank too much to drive home safely.

Mom's father, John Peter Leaf, was a pastor and an outspoken prohibitionist. Mom more than once told us of a time in her teens when a group of men gathered one night outside their house porch in Tennessee Ridge. They were carrying torches, drinking, and hollering for Pastor Leaf. Morfar, my mother's father, wanted to confront them, but his wife restrained him. She felt a confrontation unwise.

After an hour or two, the group slowly broke up without incident.

January 19 [JAN 20 3 – PM]

Dear Walter,

Finally, I am getting a chance to write to you. I have been so busy writing exams, but I just couldn't seem to concentrate the way I should because I kept thinking about you and the little home. I can hardly wait to see the pictures. Then another thing I am still fighting that same cold. Last night Tick, Helen and I worked up at school until after midnight. I was over to Thorsons with one of my tests to have him check it. He gave me a pint of wine to drink to keep me from coughing at night. He is surely kind to me.

I'm not sure Margaret drank any of that wine. During my early years, Mom was averse to drinking alcohol in pretty much any form except for the Mogen David wine used in the Lutheran communion service.

Years later, Mom visited my family's home. Mom didn't sleep well because of a persistent tickle in her chest that made her cough. The next evening she asked if I had any cough syrup. I said, "Sure. I have one that works well for me." It was an equal mixture of cherry cough syrup and Cointreau. It stopped the tickle and Mom slept well.

She repeated her request the following night. The next day she was feeling much better after sleeping well again, so I asked her, "Want to know what's in it?"

She shook her head no.

Soon we start on our contest numbers. Mr. Thorson plans to send for them. Really, I am getting spoiled because it seems I get out of doing so many things. There came a dun from the state library of $1.10. I showed it to Mr. Thorson and right away he said, "Don't worry about that I'll take care of that today." He offered to run off my stencils, too. I hope I can do something to repay him a little.

The President's Ball is soon here. Some students wanted to sell me a ticket; I refused. Helen asked me later if I had been asked. I answered, "Yes." but said that I refused. She told me that I didn't need to get a ticket but just donate the money. I asked her how much. She said, "twenty-five cents." I haven't given any and do not plan to.

Walter, I think it not Christian to have a ball to help the children who have infantile paralysis. I plan to send some money to Bethphage and ask them to use it for the children who are thus handicapped. It seems to me that of having a dance is the world's and the devil's way of sacrificing. May God make me to know how to give gifts to the sick and the poor.

The other evening I was invited to a party sponsored by the Kill Kare Klub. The girls wouldn't let me go because of my cough. Afterwards, I learned that the time at the party had been spent on sewing cotton snowballs for the President's ball. Oh, I was so thankful that I hadn't gone. They[,] the decorating committee, are making 1050 snowballs for the occasion. Tonight a group is busy working on them. Wouldn't it be wiser if they used their time in a better manner to help the helpless paraletics? What do you think?

Walter, I wish I could tell you how happy I am that I got to be with you this Christmas. May god ever guide us. I wish I were a more able person but what I have that I give to you. Every day that we are together in our home you will have to overlook mistakes and my faults but I am sure that when night comes you will forgive me and then in the morning we can start out in a new and bright way. Jesus forgives me daily and I know you love Him and want to follow in His footsteps so you will forgive, although, I know, it will be very difficult sometimes.

Lovingly,

Margaret

Although moral issues and values vary with time and culture, they are not monolithic. Here Margaret struggled with dancing. What might have her struggle been like had she been teaching high school in Nazi Germany where the social pressure to conform was staggering?

Jan. 22 [JAN 22 ?PM]

My Dear Margaret:

In all thy ways acknowledge him. And he will direct thy paths. Proverbs 3:6.

Margaret: May God forbid that I ever cease to thank him, for directing my path to you. In your last letter, you mentioned that I might burn it, if I wanted to. I'll never burn it. Margaret; I often feel just as you said you do and I wish that you were here so you could comb my hair and I could hold you close and rumple your hair just a little, in fact I need a shampoo and it seems I will have to give it to myself. . . . Shall we make a resolution; that whenever we feel lonely for one another, we will instead, pray for our future. Our marriage, our home, our children and our friends always leaving all to Jesus, in his care and subject to his will.

Margaret I wish I might have put a ring on your finger, Christmas eve. Had I been financially able, I would not have had one to put on, for I never dreamed that you could care for me. I only hoped and prayed and I just couldn't keep from asking if I might come. Again I thank god for his direction. It would be nice though, If you had a ring and God willing you shall have one as soon as he lets me have the means to get it. It is also hard for me not to tell everyone. I have slipped some, but some, even thought I would bring you with me. I guess the little birdies carried the messages.

2 p.m.

By the way; I received the very nicest letter from North Dakota, from a very dear girl; Miss Margaret Leaf. Margaret, I must confess that I long, Oh so much! To see you and then I would like to squeeze you real hard, just to know that it was all real. Your letters are encouraging. They just seem to lift me up and make all tasks seem light.

Margaret it may be God's will, that we should not see each other for such a long time, so be, always, of good cheer and when you feel lonely, talk and walk with God. Ask him to make of me a worthy husband, to teach me how to love, to forgive and forget, to give and give and ask for these same things for yourself and our home. What a glorious home it will be, with Christ, for the cornerstone and the ever present guest.

My dear, you speak of your faults, but remember; that for at least every fault of yours, needing forgiving I have one and probably more. I am not perfect. That is why I marvel that you care for me at all.

Now about some questions in your last letter. Why not; if we wish to help paralytics, dig down in our pockets and help them, then go to bed at 8 o'clock at night, instead of from 1 to 6 in the morning, so that we will be fitted to earn more for them and God, to whom they belong?

Getting at the truth in all of its ramifications is seldom simple, especially when wanting to grow the spirit of a marital relationship. The process is like kindling and building a fire with sticks and logs of truth. While you want to share your whole truth, the elements of that truth are often best shared in a manner that carefully fuels rather than smothers the fire.

Walter could have agreed with Margaret that the prince of sinister spirits was urging the Washburn community to organize the President's Ball. He didn't, even though on December 5, he described the power of the devil and suggested that spirit's likely presence in "the continual round of parties, dances, and clubs and theaters."

Although Walter didn't sense a sinister spirit at work in the community, he believed that helping paralytics was ancillary to the community's primary goal of having a grand ball. He may have been right, but would the community dig deep in their pockets if a Presidential Ball were not held? Walter observed in his October 30 letter that sometimes morally compelling duties "become a joy and are a joy but not always." The Washburn community may have found a joy-filled way of helping paralytics.

By the way Margaret; I'm a punk night hawk. I need lots of sleep. In my work especially during spring, summer and fall, it is necessary to rise early and work quite long hours. It makes you tired, a healthy tired feeling which makes you sleep well. You speak or rather question if we; will rise early. My dear; I cannot tell you how happy I will be, if you would rise early with me. Then to kneel beside our bed and ask God to walk with us thru the day. Then a few moments together in His word and I would go to the chore duties while you prepare breakfast. Is that what you meant? I have dreamt of it and that is why you are the only girl whom I ever held in my arms. I knew she must be a Christian and I thank God for directing my path and answering my prayer.

About rolled grain, horses and various farm problems, never fear or worry. You shall soon know about them, for my Margaret is going to be with me, to feed, haul hay and grain and many other things. We shall plan our work so as to be together as much as possible, even though we live on the farm shall we not?

Now with much love, I ask God to keep you and bless you.

Yours in Christ.

Walter.

In her November 11 letter, Margaret envisioned "a family who has the Unseen Guest always in their home."

Walter had a similar thought. This raises a question. How can something be present if not materially present?

The brain is a complex web of intricately connected neurons. Thoughts arise through a complex exchange of signaling chemicals called neurotransmitters. Some such neural flashing evoked the thought of an "unseen guest" in Margaret. She transcribed these thoughts into patterns of ink on her letter. When Walter opened that letter, rays of light reflected off those ink patterns and entered Walter's interpretive eye. Through an analogous exchange of neurotransmitters in Walter's brain, the thought of Margaret's "unseen guest" also appeared in Walter's mind.

Walter responded. The sense of his concurring thoughts was transformed into arm and finger movements that created the ink patterns on his letter to Margaret. A couple of days later, other light rays reflected off those ink patterns and entered Margaret's mind through her interpretive eye. She learned that the "unseen guest" was now in both of their minds, even though without the "eye" of a scientist, she may have believed the "unseen guest" was spiritually, but not materially present.

Jesus cogently phrases the matter of his material presence in Matthew 18:20, "For where two or three are gathered in my name, there am I in the midst of them." That being the case, who knows what unseen guests become materially present in our homes and offices through our words, gestures, and actions?

January 22 [JAN 24 7 AM]

Dear Walter,

"And Jehovah, he it is that doth go before thee; He will be with thee, he will not fail thee, neither forsake thee: fear not, neither be dismayed." Deuteronomy 31: 8.

This was one of the verses that I read for devotions today. It was given by Moses to Joshua and now I wish to give it to you. It has been extended to me by mother and father many a time but it stands just as forcibly and powerfully now as when Moses gave it for the first time. Walter, I wouldn't enjoy writing letters if I couldn't write anything spiritual because that is the only thing that is lasting through time and eternity.

Thanks for the pictures. I didn't realize that the house you were speaking about looked so new and modern. I can visualize somewhat how much the green vegetation and flowers would add in beautifying the surroundings. I can hardly wait to see the plan of the interior of the house. . . . I am glad there are so many trees on the place. The trees in front of Browns' large home look beautiful. The little home must be light and easily ventilated since it has so many windows.

This morning after Sunday School Pastor Berg asked me to resume charge of directing the Junior Choir. I told him they did not seem to learn to sing when I was directing them and, besides that, it seemed I didn't have time to choose suitable numbers for them to learn. He said he would help with the getting of music and as for teaching them he hadn't seemed to be getting any place either. He said a man's voice was really too low and gruff to help those youngsters to sing. Then too, he is directing three vocal groups and to take a fourth makes it impossible to do any part well. I promised him I would take charge.

In his October 25 letter, Walter wrote, "There is time enough to assume more tasks." That time has evidently come for Margaret.

I can hardly realize that I maybe will have the chance to live with you in that cute house. It is all right that all modern conveniences are not in the home. Now we have something to look forward to when you build a home that will really belong to us. Sometime I get so thrilled to think that you love [me] even though I am not just exactly what you would like me to be or the one whom you would really want for a wife. With God's help I will be able to help you and be a joy to you because I do love you. . . . I am glad you love to travel. My father used to enjoy it a lot. I hope that I can help you pack your suitcase. If it happens that for some reason both of us couldn't go I hope to keep the home waiting for you. May God richly bless you in your work and leisure. When God wills it, may we be united in marriage.

Yours in Christian love,

Margaret

P.S. At supper this evening Tick just teased me so much about religion. I finally told him that I knew he just talked in such a manner to see how I would take it because I knew that underneath it all he thought differently than he was speaking. After that he stopped. I guess they think I am too serious but time, words and deeds are all important to me because I feel that God wants those for Him.

Regarding Margaret's interest in writing something spiritual because it would last "through time and eternity," I'm prone to say, "Right on!" That said, who truly knows what words and deeds stick in our minds and what role they will play?

Take baseball. It became a lettered sport at Eaton where I was a sophomore in high school. My brothers and I tried and, like all the hopefuls, made the team. I warmed the bench my sophomore and junior years. No problem. I loved baseball. I played during practice and enjoyed hanging out with the team.

That summer some parents and Russ Harrach, a new coach, organized an American Legion baseball team for boys sixteen and under. The occasional nights when we played away games under the lights were a special treat. We stopped for hamburgers, shakes, and fries after each game. The attending parents shared the cost for players like me whose parents had other priorities and commitments. That generosity started me thinking of the many ways this world is made better that have little to do with church.

The following spring, Russ Harrach became the high school baseball coach. During spring practice, James, my next older brother, played shortstop. Alan Beede, a sophomore, and I switched off at second base. Capability wise, it may have been a toss-up; however, it was my senior year, and I anticipated playing alongside my brother. My hopes for lettering in baseball sank when Alan was called to lead off the batting order. I recalled only one case during the preceding summer when Coach Harrach changed the starting lineup; he dropped our third and fourth hitters from the team because they skipped a game to attend a party.

To my surprise, I was called to lead off the last game of the season. We were playing Fort Lupton. James and I knew the opposing pitcher. He had good control and liked throwing overhead fast balls that usually sailed over the opposing bats.

Being a prepubescent sixteen year old, weighing a hundred five pounds and only an inch and a half over five feet, the outfielders understandably closed way in when I walked to the batter's box. As expected, the pitcher wound up and sent an overhead fast ball down the chute. I stepped in and lined it over the shortstop's head and between the outfielders for a stand-up double. My next time up, the pitcher and I had the same thing on our minds — an overhead fast ball. This time I lined it over the left fielder for another grinning double.

After the game, Coach Harrach approached me and apologized for not playing me during the season. He explained that he had played Alan so as to have a stronger team next year. I didn't know what to say. Something like "That's OK" probably came out.

I learned many things playing baseball. I learned to value the generosity of those team parents — the Basses, Blehms, Harrachs, Nelsons, and Springstons. I saw the courage and strength revealed in Coach Harrach's self-effacing apology, and I learned the importance of letting everyone have a chance to play. Just how much the spirit of generosity, the desire for reconciliation, and the importance of a rewarded effort grow each time they are experienced is for the source of yours and my being to say, for it is through people that they either flourish or fade.

A GLIMPSE BACK

*J*anuary 7. Walter was clearly surprised and elated that Margaret had walked into his life. Surprise and elation at finding a soulmate are cherished memories of many couples. What understandings do you invoke to explain the frequency of these unique relationships?

January 11. Margaret found a promise to farmers that no doubt meant a lot to Walter. Where do you look for life promises that mean a lot for you?

January 13. What understandings were at play in Walter's approach to solving the trampoline problem by casting himself upon Jesus "without any reservation whatsoever?" What understandings help you to let go of your worries or keep you from doing so?

January 16. What feelings might have swept over Margaret when she first learned she was not invited to the bridge party? Can you recall a time that you felt left out, but eventually appreciated that you were?

January 19. What social pressures do you sense Margaret encountered as a result of the President's Ball? In what ways are they similar to the social pressures affecting your choices and actions?

January 22. Walter wanted to squeeze Margaret to know "that it was all real." Her letter helped. Have you ever felt close to someone you loved, but who was not visually present? What evoked that feeling for you?

January 22. What were your first reactions to Margaret's statement about the only thing that lasts forever? What things have a lasting effect on you? What aspects, if any, of these things last forever?

NEVER MARRY A NORWEGIAN FARMER

*I*n early February, readers of the Washburn Leader learned that the "President's Ball was a complete success." Readers of the Greely Tribune were informed that 800 million was "declared inadequate for the navy."

Jan. 26, 8.20 P.M. [JAN 27 430PM]

Dear Margaret:

"Be still and know that I am God; I will be exalted among the nations, I will be exalted in the earth." Ps. 46:10.

Last Monday, I went with father and mother to Greeley, to see my banker, because I had a note coming due within a few days. I was also getting pretty low in cash and thought I could borrow a few dollars for a while, until I sold the cattle or some potatoes. The banker promised to renew the note for a time, but I could tell by his manner that it would be useless to ask for any more money, before I had paid up what I already owe. I came away feeling quite blue and it took nearly all day to dispel the feeling. When I got home I got in

my car and drove up to my place to sort potatoes. It is very quite
[quiet] there, so I could and did have a good talk, with God. I came
home feeling much better and today the gloom was displaced by
good cheer. . . . Then tonight, as I walked home "sometimes I walk
forth and back." It was very quite [quiet] and I beheld the most
beautiful sunset. It was then that the first part of this verse above,
came to me. I could readily see God's handiwork around me and I
know he was near looking after his own. Even as it says in the
verse you sent.

Walter's folks went with him to the bank, but, evidently,
were reluctant to provide further financial backing. When
Walter returned home, he headed for the dugout to sort
potatoes. Once he acclimated to the soft shuttling of the
sorter, he found the needed solitude for "a good talk, with
God." Maybe he confessed his difficulty to a presence deep
within himself. Whatever he did, it too was a form of
prayer, for we read in Romans 8:26: "Likewise the Spirit
helps us in our weakness; for we do not know how to pray
as we ought, but the Spirit himself intercedes for us with
sighs too deep for words." A few hours later, Walter walked
out of the dugout and headed home feeling much better. The
next day, his spirits were brighter. The following
Wednesday night he beheld a beautiful sunset that brought

to mind the verse he quotes. This, and other similar experiences, must figure into Walter's confidence that God answers prayers.

Margaret; I am so glad and happy that you are serious; that you feel as you said "time, words and deeds are all important to me, because I feel that God wants those for him." Tonight as I walked home I could not help marveling, that God could want one such as I. It was so good to know that he does and I thanked him for it, as I walked along. If it be his will, may he haste the day when we may enjoy sunsets and fellowship with him, together.

Since it is your wish and mine; to serve him, "Our Master", with heart soul and mind and we continually make this known unto him, thru prayer, I am sure, that we can do just that very thing. Then he will also bless our home. God must come first in our lives. He must come before me in your life and before you in mine and strangely enough if he does, each will be more dear to the other because of the love of God in us.

There are many allegiances in life: self, family, community, country, an earthly or heavenly ruler, even a way of being or of seeing the world. Walter felt that if his principal allegiance came before Margaret in his life and vice versa, they would "be more dear to the other" — a paradox to say the least, and highly dependent on the nature of their principal allegiances.

My frostbite is soon gone and I feel tip top, so I soon can take a picture or have it taken and send to you, if I can rake up the necessary money. I tied up all the little I have in feed for the cattle, so until I sell them or some potatoes it will be necessary for me to be careful of my pennies. In fact, I am going to be pretty stingy this coming summer, in order to prepare for you coming. We may not need much but we do need some and if it is Gods will that I get good crops and prices, I shall make every effort to take care of it to the furtherance of his kingdom. I am asking his help in this and know that you will do the same.

And now listen to me; young lady. I would never have gone to Minn., If I had not wanted you for my wife. I may not know all the duties of a good wife but I know most of them and I do not know one that you cannot meet to a Tee. One duty of a good wife, is to pray for her husband and I know that you already do that, even though it is not yet my privilege to be your husband. That is also the husbands duty. Margaret I know that God will help us to be a joy to each other. We have only one worry; To humbly approach him every day. Matt. 18: 3,4.

Now may God keep you and bless you and make his face shine upon you, now and forever.

Yours in Christ,

Walter

Margaret may have learned of Walter's being in debt when she was with him over the Christmas holiday. If not, she has now.

In talking about money, Walter didn't need much, but he needed some. In talking about their relationship, he needed prayer. After raising these needs, he drew her attention to Matthew 18:3-4 where Jesus says: "Truly, I say to you, unless you turn and become like children, you will never enter the kingdom of heaven. Whoever humbles himself like this child, he is the greatest in the kingdom of heaven." Walter feels that the key to his joy lies in experiencing a certain type of kingdom on earth with a child's dependent confidence.

It is not a new key, and Jesus was not the first to describe it. In Lin Yutang's translation of strophe 10 of the Tao Te Ching this understanding was voiced at least five hundred years earlier when Lao Tzu said, "In embracing the One with your soul, can you never forsake the Tao? In controlling your vital force to achieve gentleness, can you become like the new-born child?"

My awareness of Dad's being in debt first arose when I was in the third or fourth grade. One day while rummaging in his desk I leafed through his checkbook. Nothing particularly interested me at first, just checks for groceries, clothes, tools, and such, until I noticed the balance was running out. Then it increased as a result of selling some beans. The next jump in the otherwise diminishing balance was a bank loan. I leafed faster looking for and finding more loans. I already knew we did not have much money. By the time I closed the checkbook, a troubling awareness had taken root; we owed money.

January 30 [JAN 31 3 – PM]

My dear Walter,

"Speak, Jehovah; for They servant heareth" I Sam. 3:9

"Hitherto hath Jehovah helped us" I Sam. 7:12

Thanks for the letter I received yesterday. I feel sorry that you are low on funds. Don't worry about buying the ring now. I prefer not having one that would be charged. If God wills that you get a good price for your cattle, He will give it to you. I know what it means to have to live on very little, but, someway, it all turns out well.

Helen is going to heat some soup for my supper as soon as she gets home from supper. She surely is kind to me. Yesterday she bought a bed lamp so that we can read at night. It seems I am trying not to get into debt but instead save money so that I don't buy such things. I am planning to put $30 on savings account each month. I really have enough clothes.

Walter, you guessed right when you wondered if I meant to awaken early. I love to get up in the mornings. We have always done that at home ever since I can remember of getting up. All of us were at the breakfast table together but then us girls would sleep some in the afternoon after the dishes were done. I'll be glad to prepare breakfast while you are out doing the chores. Helen said she would never marry a Norwegian farmer because they always make the womenfolk do the chores. I told her I could hardly believe it. Well, she said that's because I knew so little about farm life. She said her father was English so that was the reason the womenfolk at her home didn't have to do the chores while the men were sitting around reading and smoking. I told her that you said that you didn't believe a woman should do the chores. She said she supposed then that Swedes were different from Norwegians.

The Eng. IV class have made poetry booklets. One pupil drew pictures to illustrate the poems. All these poems were to be taken from current magazines and the daily newspapers. They were to identify the poems as to type such as: epic, elegy, ode, metrical tale, etc. Another pupil, Carol Wilson, wrote a three stanza poem dedicating the booklet to me. That's the first time a pupil has ever written a poem to me that I know of.

I am glad that Mr. Heard has not left yet. I hate to think of your staying all alone during these cold months. I hope that your back will be strong now. May God bless and keep you ever His.

Yours in Christian love,

Margaret

Margaret's saving reminds me of the time we needed to replace our musty 1937 Ford into which at least six of us kids piled into the back seat on family outings. Mom got out a big jar. We put our loose change in it. Within a few months the jar was half full. When she remarked, "See, we already have enough for the steering wheel," the thought crossed my mind, "We're never going to get a new car."

Still, the lesson was there. In high school I found a systematic way of saving money for fishing tackle. We were given $1.25 a week to buy cafeteria tickets for lunch. At the pool hall I could pick up a hot dog and Coke for fifteen cents and squirrel away the other ten. I eventually acquired a metal tackle box, a fly book, a few wet flies, a streamer, and some other small items with the money I saved.

I wasn't looking forward to explaining where I got the money for purchases when we climbed out of the car to rig up our poles on opening day of the next fishing season. I needn't have worried. After Dad commented that he liked my tackle box, he said, "We had better get started; the fish are already feeding."

Jan. 31 [JAN 31 230 PM

Dear Margaret:

"If ye abide in me, and my words abide in you, ask whatsoever ye will, and it shall be done unto you." John 15:7.

This is somehow a very hard letter to get started upon. My greeting to you will be: that the Grace and Peace of our Lord and Savior may be yours today and always. Are you well and completely recovered from your cold now?

I still sort potatoes and haul bedding and feed for my cattle. It seems I am busy all the time yet I get so very little done. There are books to be ordered for the S. S. and songs to pick out and quite a few other things to do. You see I need a wife very much. I am so glad that you love to go to church and work in the church, Margaret. That you do pray and seek the power that only He can give. That I can write to you about these things. It will be such a help and such a joy to share my burdens and all else that I have with you. It felt so natural and easy to kneel in prayer with you and even though now, that cannot be, it helps me, to know, that you are praying for me and for the time, when we may establish our home.

Sometimes I get kind of blue because of the financial conditions of the country and the general outlook on the livestock and produce market. It is then, such promises as the one in John

15:7 are a great help and consolation. And I always remember that it is indeed a mighty, kind and gracious God who directs our paths.

Yours in Christ,

Walter

February 1 [FEB 3 3 — PM]

Dear Walter,

"David strengthened himself in Jehovah his God.["] I Samuel 30:6b.

The book of Samuel which I completed reading this evening has been very interesting. I regret that I have read it so few times. David was certainly a wonderful young Christian man thru out this book. I just read the first chapter of II Samuel. I have come to the conclusion that that Amalekite who said he had killed Saul told a lie because in the first book it mentions that Saul fell upon his own sword. That lie finally caused his death because David killed him. It was, I presume, to save his good standing in David's eyes that he came to tell David. I surely realize more what it means when one speaks about God's anointed.

Say, when you get enough money to buy a diamond, would you get the ring in yellow gold instead of white. I like yellow better. Will it be fun to wear a ring! I can hardly wait to get [it] but I surely wish that you could put it on.

The English IV class have been having fun studying humorous poetry and prose and the authors' lives of the selections. Don Marquis, formerly newspaper humorist, was one of the authors mentioned. I mentioned in class that he was in charge of the Sun Dial, a section in the New York Sun. Allagene Jefferis bought a paper tonight that mentioned that Don Marquis had not written in the Sun Dial section since 1922 and that he had passed away and that a whole section was to be devoted to him. I can hardly understand how it should happen that she should get that certain copy of the paper concerning Don Marquis, but I think it is just one of the many ways that He is answering our prayers concerning my work.

Helen is busy reading Sinclair Lewis' book, Babbitt. Have you ever read it. I haven't, but my pupils have, and, consequently, I have read reports on it.

Walter, I am so glad that you think that I will be able to do what is required of a wife. With your help and God's together with help from your folks and mine I am sure I will be able, although, I was afraid I wouldn't.

Byron Dutoit joined my boys glee club today. I was in dire need of another tenor. He is a good one. Another time our prayers have been answered.

Now, you can't imagine how much fun it has been to write to you although I am sitting up in bed with the lines of my writing running almost any direction imaginable. Goodnight and God bless you always.

Lovingly,

Margaret

"Call upon Me in the day of trouble; I will deliver thee, and thou shalt glorify Me."

Thanks for the letter I received last night. I certainly will excuse your stationery. It does seem strange how a change of paper gives a different appearance to a letter. I have just enough of the stationery which Ruth gave me to write two letters to her. I have two stamps left of the ones she gave me, also.

Last night I dreamt about you. I dreamt we were on our way to see a wedding. This was to help us plan one of our own. It was fun to be with you in my dreams but — oh, will it be fun next winter? I can hardly wait.

I heard the cattle price had gone down 50¢. I don't blame you for feeling discouraged. I have not prayed much about the market price. I have never included that in my prayers that I can recall before I met you.

Lovingly, yours in Christ,
Margaret.

Helen is quite sick. Mr. Thorson doesn't want me to sleep with her because he says it is a throat trouble that is contagious. She fainted while calling Mr. Thorson about 9 o'clock.

Margaret is trying to reconcile a seeming discrepancy in the Bible regarding the death of King Saul. Here are the two troubling accounts:

I Samuel 31:4-5 reads as follows:

> *Then Saul said to his armor-bearer,*
> *"Draw your sword, and thrust me through with it, lest*
> *these uncircumcised come and thrust me through with it."*
> *But his armor-bearer would not; for he feared greatly.*
> *Therefore Saul took his own sword, and fell upon it. And*
> *when his armor-bearer saw that Saul was dead, he also fell*
> *upon his sword, and died with him.*

II Samuel 1:5-10 reads as follows:

> *Then David said to the young man who told him, "How do*
> *you know that Saul and his son Jonathan are dead?" And*
> *the young man who told him said, "By chance I happened to*
> *be on Mount Gilboa; and there was Saul leaning upon his*
> *spear; and lo, the chariots and the horsemen were close upon*
> *him. And when he looked behind him, he saw me, and called*
> *to me. And I answered, 'Here I am.' And he said to me,*
> *'Who are you?' I answered him, 'I am an Amalekite.' And*
> *he said to me, 'Stand beside me and slay me; for anguish has*
> *seized me, and yet my life still lingers.' So I stood beside*
> *him, and slew him, because I was sure that he could not live*
> *after he had fallen; and I took the crown which was on his*

head and the armlet which was on his arm, and I have
brought them here to my lord."

It is easy to agree with Margaret that the young Amalekite might curry favor by lying to David, Saul's rival for the kingship of house of Israel. Understanding Margaret's need to reconcile this discrepancy is a much deeper matter. Why do we feel every seeming discrepancy or inconsistency in our scriptures must be reconciled?

Implicit in Margaret's interest in David is a common, often unconscious concern: Who is a member of my belief group? Margaret believes David is a Christian even though he lived a thousand years before Jesus and never spoke specifically about the life and sacrifice of Jesus.

Lao Tzu, who lived roughly five hundred years before Jesus, seemingly did pay homage to the role Jesus would play. In Lin Yutan's translation of strophe 78 of the Tao Te Ching he says, "Who receives unto himself the calumny of the world is the preserver of the state. Who bears himself the sins of the world is the King of the world."

Mahomet, born roughly six hundred years after Jesus, did not notably revere Jesus's particular role of "bearing the sins of the world," but did revere Jesus as a prophet of God.

Margaret saw David as a Christian, but would she see Lao Tzu and Mohomet as Christians? Maybe not. Unlike Lao Tzu and Mahomet, David was a loved biblical figure and a forefather of Jesus.

Even though our religious distinctions are often deemed God-inspired, especially when based on our scriptures, we are not born with them. Instead we are born with a child's universal curiosity toward, and acceptance of, everyone. We are also born with or soon acquire an almost reverential awe of and love for our parents. We quickly learn to recognize the members of our parental family. That family identity is natural and fundamental, yet it does not separate us from our playmates. We are even comforted and assured in our universal identity when our family and the families of our playmates gather together.

Mom never completely lost that universal identity. Race, color, creed, social status, and all the other things on which the spirit of separation can work didn't significantly enter her personal encounters. She would quickly be caught up in the interaction, empathizing with a hurt or exhilarating in an achievement.

Her personal interactions contrasted with her distrust of the understandings and practices related to denominational beliefs that differed from hers, so I was surprised when opening a thick little day book she gave me many years later. Each page came with a Bible verse. The names of her extended family members were written on the pages corresponding to their birthdays. In the book were two slips of paper. One had a verse from the Bible printed on each side. On the other she had inked the words "Let my love, like sunlight surround you and yet give you illumined freedom. — Rabindranath Tagore."

Feb. 2 [FEB 3 830 PM]

Dear Margaret:

"The harvest indeed is plenteous, but the laborers are few."
Matt. 9:38

Today as on other days, the thought came to me that the harvest is indeed great. There are so many, many souls, yet to be garnered. Often as I work alone especially in the dugout, these thoughts come to me and appall me. I feel so unable to cope with the problem. Then as I look at this verse I find the answer to the problem, in the verse following, in the form of a request, "Pray ye therefore the Lord of the harvest, that he send forth laborers into his harvest." It is also good to remember that all things are possible with God. In "John 4" we find he uses a sinful Samaritan woman to carry the gospel news to her people. So perhaps I too can be of some help to Jesus who has done so much and been so good to me.

You may tell Helen, If you wish that I have 3 sisters, neither of which has ever milked a cow or done any other kind of chores except as they wanted to. If, you ever do; it will be because you want to or want to be with me. I plan to help you as much as possible especially evenings, so that we will be through at the same time, and then we can both sit down and read or you may want to knit. By the way, how is the knitting coming? I also plan to arrange my work, so that I will not be so taken up as not to have time to share your plans or work around the house. I think husband and wife should share each others plans as well as their means, sorrows and joys. That is why I shall not do any more or buy any more than is necessary for the house. Then when you are here we can discuss and make plans together. Perhaps you do not know a great deal about farm life, but it seemed last summer that you were interested in things concerning it. (In fact that is one of the reasons I liked you. That and your interest in all things. Also your love of nature.) It will not take you long to learn and I plan to share my problems with you from the beginning.

Spring is coming fast. The days are already much longer. Today I saw several meadow larks and some of the perennial weeds are showing green even though the ground is icy and frozen as yet. I still sort potatoes. (It is a slow job to pick seed, that is to select, the most choice potatoes, to plant this spring.) The soil will work better this spring than for many years because of the plentiful rain and snow.

I am going to move up to my house Sat as Mr. & Mrs. Heard are leaving Friday.

Yours in Christ,

Walter.

These leaves I picked up in the entrance to the dugout. I do not know for sure what they are, but they are so beautifully colored that I thought I would send them to you. God's coloring never clashes does it?

How can an ordinary person cope with global problems? As I see it, a vast reservoir of influences stirs within each of us. Their forms are endless: thoughts, reflections, prayers, gestures, touches, withdrawals, sounds, silences, givings, takings, acceptances, rejections, intentions, attentions and inattentions. Daily we inhale and exhale influences in unconscious clouds. Our influences spread like pollen from a river oak in a spring wind. I doubt that any pollen grain falls inconsequentially to the ground. Each pollen grain probably has consequences at some granular level. Maybe it's the one that tipped the balance when you tried not to sneeze. Maybe years ago it became part of a fossil that revealed to a scientist something of its era. Maybe it met a waiting receptor whereby a seed formed and ultimately grew into a mighty oak.

I like the following story from Mark 12:14–44 where a poor widow goes her way unconscious of the fact that her gift would resonate throughout Christendom:

> And he sat down opposite the treasury, and watched the multitude putting money into the treasury. Many rich people put in large sums. And a poor widow came, and put in two copper coins, which make a penny. And he called his disciples to him, and said to

them, "Truly, I say to you, this poor widow has put in more than all those who are contributing to the treasury. For they all contributed out of their abundance; but she out of her poverty has put in everything she had, her whole living."

The consequences of our influences spring up wherever we go. They are present before we arrive and linger after we leave. They cross continents and oceans at ever-increasing speeds and are already venturing into space. They knit us into others and others into us.

Because we have only a surface cognizance of the influences that define us, they are best left in the hands of the unfathomable source from which they ultimately spring and into which they inevitably return. When so left, we are free to focus on the spirit and nature of our daily walk.

February 5 [FEB 7 3 – PM]

Dear Walter,

We got our checks this morning. I don't believe that I have told you what my salary is. I get one hundred dollars a month. I put thirty dollars in savings account. I don't have a checking account. Formerly I have sent quite a lot home but they don't want me to do so now as they want me to save for my own use later if I can possibly put some aside. I plan to send at least twenty dollars to pay for church dues and house rent. I don't know if the folks will accept the money for house rent. In that case I plan to have them use it for the Clarissa Church building fund. Ebba, mother, and I pledged $100 to be paid within three years and I want to pay at least forty dollars before May.

I told Helen about your three sisters. She said, "That is certainly different than in my community." She said also that her mother was the only Norwegian mother in her locality that didn't do field work and chores. Walter, I believe you when you say that we will help one another. I do so want to help you and I need as much help all the time that that is why I am afraid you will be disappointed in me but then I am praying God to give me wisdom and strength to do that which He wants me to do in the years to come.

Walter, I am glad that you are a farmer. Farmers can do so much for humanity. My father's and mother's folks were farmers

*and here none of their children have lived on the farm so I think
that maybe I am the one that should. Really, I don't care much for
living in town. It will be fun to see things grow. Just think if we
were living in the time of pioneering it would be entirely different.
Stock might be cheap now but think how hard it is for other
business men to make a living. There are very few callings of today
that is as honest and honorable as farming. The teaching field is
certainly not safe and secure. Some teachers receive only warrants
which are difficult to get cashed and when cashed must get it at
less than full value.*

*Today you were to move to your home. I bet you are tired
tonight. I hope that you will soon be able to send me another plan
of the house. I hope we can get a piano as soon as possible. You
know you want to learn to play and I want to be your teacher. I
have enough music books to keep you busy. I want to play too.
When your sister Mabel comes you know we will want to hear her
play. Evodia and she can play duets together. Won't it be fun
though? . . .*

    Yours in Him,

    Margaret

    *It is too bad that the stock market has gone down. I don't
understand why it must fluctuate so much. Ebba read about the
schools in N. D. that are having to close unless the U. S.*

government gives financial aid. We don't belong to that group of
schools.

May God help you in your work and in your new
environment.

Margaret

If Margaret didn't find a way to enjoy farm life, it would not be for not trying. While looking for things to enjoy about farm life, she enlisted the heritage from both sets of her grandparents and, in her metaphoric take on life, elevated farming into a calling.

She was successful. Mom enjoyed seeing plants grow, hoeing weeds, reaching for eggs under the chickens, feeding the kittens, and hanging out wash. She didn't gripe and complain when storms and disease destroyed the crops and financial worries mounted in spite of her prayers.

A GLIMPSE BACK

January 26. In writing that Margaret and he will become dearer to each other if they put God first in their lives, Walter posed a paradox: What allegiance held by two people can be more important to their relationship than their allegiance to each other? Have you an allegiance that answers that paradox for your most critical relationship with another person? What is it about the nature of your allegiance that makes it a fitting answer for you?

January 31. How would you characterize what Walter enjoys about Margaret? How would you characterize what you enjoy or would enjoy in a soul mate?

Febuary 1. Do you feel a part of a belief group? How far back in time does it extend? Who do you include? Who do you exclude?

AFTERWORD

The courtship letters of Walter and Margaret comprise the first third of their premarital correspondence. Their courtship had a few rough edges, but rather quickly gave rise to mutual visions of spiritual harmony. They shared a sense of a heavenly father caring for them and responding to their thoughts and prayers.

However, in addition to the deteriorating world outlook in the newspaper headlines, the last two letters presaged some coming personal struggles: Walter's banker was not encouraging; Margaret began taking note of the livestock market. Those struggles materialized in their winter letters, the next installment of their growing love for each other, a period in which their faith in God was tested and their future together was questioned as they sought a deeper understanding of their joy in each other.

ACKNOWLEDGMENTS

I cannot know, but would like to thank all who have
contributed to this book, if only through interest and
conversation. Lois Barliant painstakingly scanned the letters
into a PDF file. Claire Barliant suggested a timeline of world
events. Helene Leaf provided much of the historical material
on Margaret's parents and grandparents. Paul Johnson
translated the Swedish expressions. The Washburn Leader
staff graciously let me browse their archived newspapers.
Diane Shepard suggested adding the self-exploratory
questions. My brothers and sisters, Mary, Paul, James, Lois,
Ruth, Caleb and Anna provided helpful recollections of our
childhood experiences. The suggestions of Lois, Anna,
Garrett Boersma, Sandra Edwards, Forman Friend, Dyan
Horowitz, David Pierce, Lynn Rix and other members of the
First Coast Christian Writers, Kimberly Smith of KM Smith
Writes, and Diane Shepard particularly enhanced the book's
readability. Bill Fleming, my long-time friend, helpfully
criticized early versions of the manuscript; Diane Worden of

Wordendex Plus, Diane Shepard, and Bobbie Christmas of Zebra Communicaitons very helpfully copy-edited later versions. Martha, my loving life companion, patiently read and carefully critiqued the many drafts while lovingly supporting the drawn-out effort from beginning to end. My thanks to all and especially to her.

ABOUT THE AUTHOR

*M*ark Johnson has published numerous scientific papers and coedited the book *Concepts and Applications of Molecular Similarity*. He has been an elder at a large Lutheran church and a large Reformed church. As a seeker, he has experienced spiritually transformative moments. As a scientist and lay theologian, he has delved into the complementarities of religious and scientific truths. To learn more, visit him at www.findyourtuningfork.com.

www.ingramcontent.com/pod-product-compliance
Lightning Source LLC
Chambersburg PA
CBHW061719020426
42331CB00006B/998